DIG IT!
ARCHAEOLOGY FOR KIDS

CAITLIN SOCKIN

PERSNICKETY PRESS

Dear Parents,

For many of us, the word "archaeology" evokes images of Indiana Jones running through jungles, jumping off planes, and fist-fighting in exotic, far-flung places. But in real life, archaeology is a far more complex endeavor than Jones' fictional adventures. Even his well-known phrase ("It belongs in a museum!") does not, in fact, reflect international protocols for the preservation of archaeological remains.

As Caitlin Sockin explains in this delightful new book, the study of the past requires careful consideration of different types of evidence, ranging from small, carbonized plant seeds to hulking architectural remains. Moreover, the question of who owns the materials that are unearthed by archaeologists is much more complicated than Hollywood would make it seem.

But, for all its complexity, archaeology is also eminently accessible. To become an archaeologist, all you really need is to be curious about the world around you and know how to look. Sockin is an expert guide to the many layers of archaeological practice. *Dig It! Archaeology for Kids* introduces readers both to what archaeologists do and how they work. It also invites readers to explore key archaeological sites in Europe, Asia, Australia, and the Americas.

Thoroughly researched and beautifully illustrated, Sockin's book offers us a chance to travel through time and space, while teaching us how to look and think like an archaeologist. Each section of this book and the hands-on activities developed by the author will be great fun for the whole family. *Dig It! Archaeology for Kids* will inspire children of all ages to look at their surroundings anew and start exploring whether they are at the beach, on the mountains, or in their own neighborhoods.

Hérica Valladares, Book Contributor
Associate Professor of Classics, University of North Carolina at Chapel Hill

Dear Educators,

This book is designed to introduce readers to the exciting field of archaeology through an engaging and interactive approach that meets students where they are and encourages them to dive deeper using their smartphones or other devices. Content is presented in an approachable way emphasizing the excitement of exploring the physical remains of the past and their relevance in the present world. The layout of the book presents the tools, methods, and ideas archaeologists use to explore the past in their own unique way and introduces readers to the controversies and contributions of archaeology to understanding human history. Readers are exposed to practical concerns like where archaeologists are employed and how to join a "dig," as well as fun activities and links to appropriate web content reinforcing core concepts.

Through a series of case studies, the book also highlights some of the remarkable and powerful physical objects that make up the archaeological record. The case studies have been carefully chosen to highlight the fact that every region of the world has an exciting history worthy of exploration and respect. Each of these can be visually explored by following QR codes embedded throughout the book. These case studies can be paired with more detailed examination of the geography, history, cultures, and languages of each region to help students understand the broader context of each case study (i.e., what is happening in different places and times).

In fact, educators are encouraged to supplement each section of this book with complementary questions and content. For example, archaeology is not the only way to explore the past. How else can students talk and know about the past? Answers to this question could include reference to other school disciplines like history and STEM but also the oral traditions and family histories passed on by our elders. In short, this book provides an accessible and engaging entry point to talk with students about the peoples and objects of the past in an ethically positive and technically accurate way.

Benjamin S. Arbuckle, Book Contributor
Professor of Anthropology, University of North Carolina at Chapel Hill

TABLE OF CONTENTS

How to Use this Book 6-7

Imagine that you are standing in a... 8-9

What is Archaeology? 10-15

Archaeology Steps 16-49

• Get the Lay of the Land (Site) 18-21

• Now Dig a Little Deeper (Excavation) 22-28

• Keep Tabs on the Lab (Lab Work) 29-37

• Tell the Story (Interpretation) 38-45

• Keep the Past Alive (What Happens Next?) 46-49

Lost and Found (Weather, Nature, and Erosion) 50-57

Stories Untold (Household Archaeology) 58-59

Words Left Behind (Archaeology and History) 60-63

Art Left Behind (Archaeology and Art History) 64-67

Outstanding in Their Fields (Types of Archaeologists) 68-75

Archaeology and You! 76-79

• Become an Archaeologist 76-77

• Where Do Archaeologists Work? (Careers) 78-79

Archaeology is a BIG Deal! 80-85

Additional Resources / Activities 86-91

Glossary 92-95

Bibliography 96-97

Acknowledgments 97

Photo and QR Code Credits 98-99

Great Zimbabwe in Zimbabwe, Africa

Pompeii in Italy, Europe

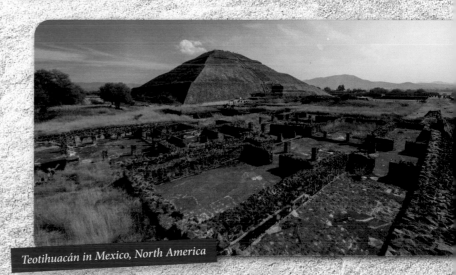
Teotihuacán in Mexico, North America

Introduction / Foreword and Edited by Dr. Benjamin Arbuckle and Dr. Hérica Valladares

Designed and edited by Brian Scott Sockin

Edited by Deborah Lee Rose

ISBN: 978-1-943978-61-8

Printed in China
cpsia tracking label information
Production Location: Rightol, China
Production Date: 12/12/2022
Cohort: Batch No. F2C0163547

10 9 8 7 6 5 4 3 2 1

Produced by Persnickety Press
An imprint of WunderMill, inc.
321 Glen Echo Lane, Suite C
Cary, NC 27518

www.WunderMillBooks.com

For my parents, who encourage me to pursue fields of interest—such as writing and archaeology—and inspire me to be creative.

DIG IT!
ARCHAEOLOGY FOR KIDS

How to Use this Book

Words and Definitions

You will learn many new words on your journey through this book. The first time you see a new word or term in a sentence or paragraph that is **bold, blue, and underlined**, it is defined right in the sentence or paragraph that you're reading.

The first time you see a new word or term that is **bold, black, and underlined** on a journal page for an archaeological site, you'll find it's definition in an orange side bar with a trowel icon under "**Words to Remember**."

All words/terms in **blue** or **black** are also defined at the back of the book in the Glossary.

QR Code Videos

SCAN FOR VIDEO

Experience what it's like to be at a famous archaeological location or dig site! Hover a smartphone camera over any QR code.

Then click the link that pops up and you will be transported to an amazing video (above) or activity website (left).

Archaeological Sites

Throughout *DIG IT!*, you'll find amazing archaeological discoveries that help us better understand the past.

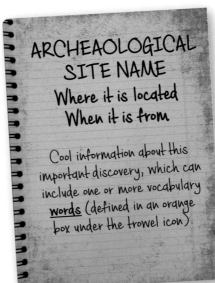

ARCHAEOLOGICAL SITE NAME
Where it is located
When it is from

Cool information about this important discovery, which can include one or more vocabulary words (defined in an orange box under the trowel icon).

Each groundbreaking discovery will be on a journal page (left) showing what it's called, where it's located, and when certain people lived there. You can also view all the sites on the map and timeline on the *DIG IT!* inside covers.

SITE NAME
Words to Remember

Word: definition
example

LET'S GET STARTED AND TRAVEL THE WORLD *THROUGH TIME...*

How We Label Time

There are many ways to label time. Here's how we measure it in this book:

- **CE (Common Era)**: This is the time we've been in for the past 2,000+ years, we're in right now, and we'll be in tomorrow and into the future. For example, the first human step on the moon was in 1969 CE.

- **BCE (Before the Common Era)**: This is the time before the Common Era began. The older or further back in time, the larger the date is. For example, the year before 100 BCE was 101 BCE.

- **Ancient**: Long, long ago

- **c. (Circa)**: *Around the time*, not an exact date. For example, c. 1900 CE means around the year 1900.

- **BP (Before Present)**: This is the number of years ago. For example, 50 BP means 50 years ago. In this book, we calculate BP dates going backward from the year 2000 CE.

...huge stadium, cheering on your favorite competitors racing past you in horse-drawn chariots!

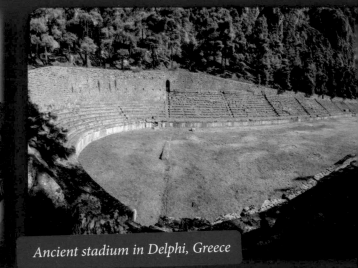
Ancient stadium in Delphi, Greece

...colorful palace, gazing at two acrobatic performers flying through the air over a bull's sharp horns!

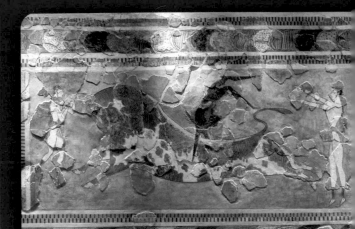
Bull-leaping fresco from Knossos, Crete

...crowded amphitheater, watching gladiators below fighting the most brutal battle of the century!

Colosseum in Rome, Italy

Long ago, humans were in these places and did these things. They lived different lives than we do now, yet similar in many ways. Like chariot racing back then, today people watch the Olympics. Like bull-leaping back then, today people watch bullfighting. And like gladiator battles back then, today people watch professional boxing.

What if you could hop into a **time machine** and travel back in history to see what life was REALLY LIKE hundreds and thousands of years ago?

With the help of objects left behind by people that ARCHAEOLOGISTS find today, *you can*.

Now, let's find out how this is possible...

What is Archaeology?

Archaeology means the study of ancient things, done by **archaeologists**. Archaeologists are *detectives* of the past, studying clues left behind by humans. Clues can be anything from lost temples and royal palaces to piles of trash and dinner leftovers. With these clues, archaeologists can piece together what life was like for people in the past that we might not otherwise know.

Archaeologists are also *storytellers*. Studying clues, they build *possible* true stories about ancient people. Some clues were left behind by humans before they invented written language to record their own histories. So, this storytelling helps us understand how ancient humans may have thought. Until someone invents an actual time machine, archaeology is the best thing we have to explore the past!

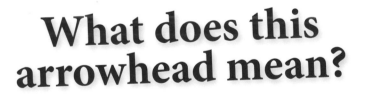

What does this arrowhead mean?

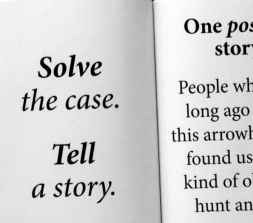

Solve the case.

Tell a story.

One *possible* story:

People who lived long ago where this arrowhead was found used this kind of object to hunt animals.

The clues that archaeologists find and study to solve the mysteries of the past fit into 3 categories: <u>artifacts</u>, <u>features</u>, and <u>ecofacts</u>.

ARTIFACTS

Hand-held objects either made or used by humans (left: jug, pins, bowl)

To find artifacts, features, and ecofacts, archaeologists need

At Machu Picchu in Peru, archaeologists found each kind of clue!

FEATURES

2

Bigger structures built by humans that cannot be easily removed (left: stone walls of buildings)

Natural things left behind by humans (right: corn, potatoes)

ECOFACTS

3

to start exploring somewhere. That somewhere is outside!

13

SCAN FOR VIDEO

MACHU PICCHU

Words to Remember

<u>**Inca Empire**</u>: the kingdom of people (Inca) in Peru, Ecuador, Bolivia, Argentina, Chile, and Colombia from c. 1400s - 1500s CE

MACHU PICCHU
Peru – South America
c. 1450 – 1550 CE (450 – 550 BP)

- The people who lived here were part of the <u>Inca Empire</u> in South America.

- The Inca Empire only lasted 100 years— a very short time period!

- People took care of llamas and ate mostly corn.

- Archaeologists think this ancient city was created for royalty.

- The Intihuatana Stone feature was placed in this city to point towards the Sun on the first day of Winter. The Inca believed this stone held the Sun on its path across the sky each year.

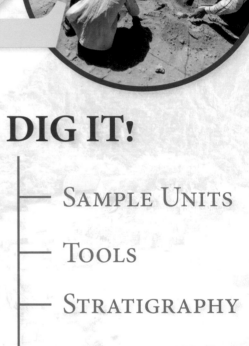

FIND A SITE

- Ground Survey
  - GPR
- Aerial Photography
- Satellite Imaging
  - LiDAR

DIG IT!

- Sample Units
- Tools
- Stratigraphy
- Excavation Code
- Backfilling

DO LAB WORK

- Clean Artifacts
- Typology
- Science Technology
  - Isotope Analysis
  - CT Scan
  - DNA Analysis
  - X-Ray Fluorescence
- Scientific Dating
  - Absolute Dating
    - Radiocarbon
    - Uranium-Series
    - Dendrochronology
  - Relative Dating
    - Stratigraphy
    - Typology

INTERPRET

- Site Analysis
- Compare and Contrast Sites

ASSIGN ARTIFACTS

- Storage
- Museums
- Return Home

To study these clues, archaeologists first need to find sites. **Sites** are places where archaeologists decide to dig artifacts, features, and ecofacts. How do archaeologists know that there is something important hidden beneath a meadow or in the middle of a jungle? Sometimes, just by chance. But usually, through technology.

Archaeologists take a survey of a potential site.

An archaeologist uses ground-penetrating radar (GPR).

On the ground, archaeologists can **survey** a potential site, walking around to look at the land to see if it's worth digging. They can also use **ground-penetrating radar (GPR)**. A GPR device sends an electric and magnetic shock down into the ground to see if it senses anything unusual buried there.

From a plane, archaeologists take photos called **aerial photographs** to get a better view of the ground below. They can also use invisible lasers, called **LiDAR**, sent from satellites that orbit Earth. These laser beams are sent down to Earth and bounce back up again to measure how high or low the ground is. The laser data create a 3D image which can reveal unexpected shapes, such as stone walls covered by a forest canopy. These walls could be part of a forgotten city!

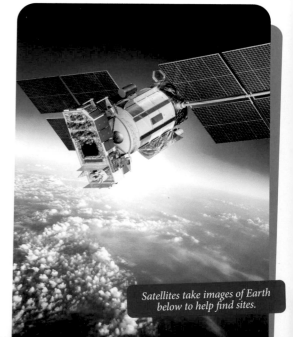

Satellites take images of Earth below to help find sites.

NAZCA LINES

Words to Remember

Geoglyphs: ground drawings

NAZCA LINES
Peru – South America
c. 400 BCE – 500 CE (1500 – 2400 BP)

Pictures taken from tall viewing towers and aerial photographs capture hundreds of <u>geoglyphs</u> down below: spirals, geometric shapes, flowers, birds, fish, monkeys, spiders, human-like figures, and other animals! Archaeologists use these photographs to map out where the ancient Nazca people drew these geoglyphs.

Aerial Photography

TIKAL
Guatemala – Central America
c. 200 – 900 CE (1100 – 1800 BP)

Unlike the Nazca Lines which you can easily see from a plane, the ancient city of Tikal is hidden among dense, rainforest trees. LiDAR helped archaeologists discover these concealed structures in the ground.

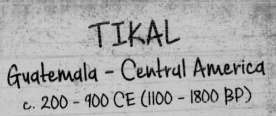

LiDAR

Once archaeologists find a site, it's time for them to get their hands a little dirty!

Monkey

Spiral

Hummingbird

Condor bird

NAZCA LINES
WHY DRAW THESE SHAPES?

Drawing over 1,000 geoglyphs known as the Nazca Lines must have taken the ancient Nazca people a lot of time and effort. So why did they do it? Some theories are that these geoglyphs were...

... waterways to catch rain or predict when it was going to rain.

... gifts to make the weather and land gods happy, since this area is known for random natural disasters.

... part of a running track.

... maps for astronomy, some lines pointing to certain stars in the galaxy.

... memorials to honor people or animals.

SCAN FOR VIDEO

An **excavation** (also called a **dig**) is the process archaeologists go through at their found site. They slowly and carefully remove layers of earth to find clues of the past.

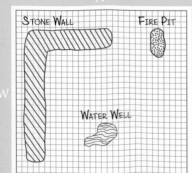

Left: A site is divided into a grid on graph paper, with features drawn across multiple units.

Archaeologists start by dividing the site into a **grid**, which is made up of side-by-side squares of land. Each square is called a **unit**. A unit is an archaeologist's assigned digging area. Using metal nails or wooden poles and rope, the unit is strung so that archaeologists don't dig outside the lines.

Archaeologists rarely dig whole sites—that would be A LOT of work. Instead, they **sample** the site by choosing units in which to dig. Just excavating these few sample units often paints a bigger picture of the full site. If there is a lot of charcoal found in all sample squares, there is likely charcoal buried in untouched units.

SCAN FOR VIDEO

The Sharpest Tools in the Shed

Shovel

SCAN FOR VIDEO

Brush

SCAN FOR VIDEO

Trowel

Bucket

Measuring Stick *Shaker screen*

Many of the things an archaeologist uses in the field are common gardening tools! Shovels are used for digging lots of dirt at once. A shaker screen separates tiny pieces of soil to reveal artifacts. Trowels and brushes carefully clear away dirt from around bigger objects in the ground to remove them safely.

Digging and Stratigraphy

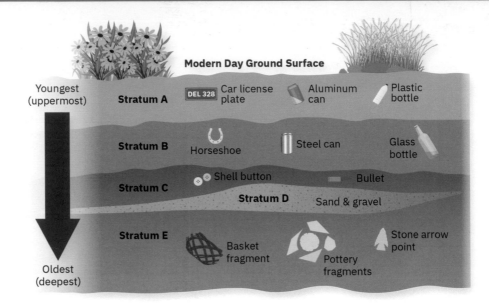

Youngest (uppermost) → Oldest (deepest)

Modern Day Ground Surface

Stratum A — DEL 328 Car license plate, Aluminum can, Plastic bottle

Stratum B — Horseshoe, Steel can, Glass bottle

Stratum C — Shell button, Bullet

Stratum D — Sand & gravel

Stratum E — Basket fragment, Pottery fragments, Stone arrow point

Archaeologists remove dirt based on **stratigraphy**. Stratigraphy is the idea that these layers of earth illustrate a timeline of the site's history. The deeper you dig, the further back in time you travel. Each layer, or **stratum**, is a time frame. For example, the first layer of earth you dig may include objects left there from 1950 - 2000 CE, while the second layer may include earlier objects from 1900 - 1950 CE.

Imagine the earth beneath your feet is a giant rainbow-layered cake, each color created with a different food coloring. A baker stacks the cake layers from the bottom color all the way up to the top color (below left, purple to red). Similarly, dirt piles up in stratigraphic layers over time (below right, light brown to dark brown).

Red ... Purple | Most recent ↑ Long ago | Dark brown ... Light brown

CAHOKIA
Words to Remember

Mound: a pyramid-like hill of dirt with a flat instead of pointed top

Mississippian Native American: describing groups who lived near the Mississippi River from c. 1000 - 1500 CE

Culture: a group of people who share parts of their lifestyle and traditions, which is how they define who they are

Mythology: stories to explain religion or culture, usually about the gods

CAHOKIA
Illinois, USA – North America
c. 1050 - 1350 CE (650 - 950 BP)

Did you know that there are pyramids in the United States? Using stratigraphy during excavation of this <u>mound</u> at Cahokia, archaeologists discovered that the <u>Mississippian Native American culture</u> built this city out of layers of sand and clay over time to reach its massive size.

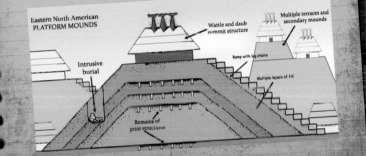

Eastern North American PLATFORM MOUNDS

Below: What Cahokia may have looked like c. 1050 - 1350 CE

SCAN FOR VIDEO

Brushing to carefully remove dirt from an artifact

Using a shaker screen

Cleaning a unit

SCAN FOR VIDEO

An achaeologist digs at each layer with a shovel and trowel. Big piles of dirt are put into shaker screens to reveal tiny artifacts hidden in the soil. Once a layer of time is removed, the unit is cleaned by scraping at the sides and bottom with a trowel until all are flat. Cleaning is done to prepare for the four steps in the excavation code...

CAHOKIA
WHY BUILD A MOUND?

Why did the Mississippian Native Americans build this mound at Cahokia back then?

Religion

Their **mythology** includes Mother Earth and Father Sky, the mound built to bring the earth closer to the sky. It was a special religious place where people came together for celebrations and feasts.

City

Like a tall skyscraper, Cahokia was the center of a big Native American population. Archaeologists found more blades, arrowheads, and axe clues here than nearby. This means the mound was a place where a lot of people lived and traded goods.

Know the Excavation Code

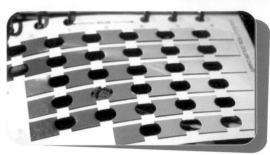

At each unit layer, archaeologists follow these FOUR STEPS:

1 Take a photograph. Include unit information on a sign and measuring sticks for reference.

2 Draw unit features on graph paper.

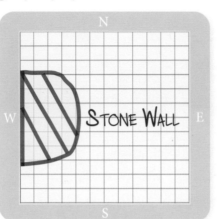

STONE WALL

3 Note the soil color. The **Munsell Chart** is an archaeology guide to figure out the color of the soil.

4 Write down the soil **texture**. The texture is how the soil feels, such as *smooth like clay* or *rough like sand*.

Dig a layer and follow the excavation code. Then do it all again! This process is repeated for each layer of time in a unit that archaeologists want to study. When they have traveled far back enough in time, archaeologists may finish the dig by shoveling the dirt back into the unit, called **backfilling**.

The work outside on the site is now done. All the artifacts are bagged, labeled, documented, and shipped off to the lab.

3 KEEP TABS ON THE LAB:
ARCHAEOLOGICAL LAB WORK

Now with these artifact clues found at the dig site, it is time to clean, sort, and apply science and technology methods.

SCAN FOR VIDEO

Archaeologists wash artifacts in buckets of water using toothbrushes.

Clay artifacts dry after cleaning.

When artifacts come out of the ground, they're covered in filth! Similar to removing gunk when brushing your teeth, most artifacts are cleaned with water and a toothbrush. Then, they're sorted into piles.

Side Notched

Corner Notched

Straight Stemmed

Contracting Stemmed

Expanding Stemmed

Triangular

Lanceolate

*Each arrowhead may have a different typology: **shape***

Archaeologists sort artifacts based on **typology**. Typology is the grouping of artifacts together that look similar—often by their design, shape, or color. Above, arrowheads can be sorted based on shape. Below, broken pieces of pottery of different colors and designs are placed into separate piles.

GREAT ZIMBABWE

Words to Remember

Shona: one of the cultural groups who live in Zimbabwe today

Ancestors: people who lived many years before you in your family or cultural group

*Pottery shards grouped by their typology: **color and design***

Archaeologists don't know everything about an artifact. Luckily, they rarely work alone! Archaeologists can call in experts for typology assistance on things like pottery, metalwork, glass, arrowheads, rocks, plants, animals, and human skeletons.

These specialists can help put together missing pieces of the archaeological puzzle. The team can then determine which cultural group of ancient people created a bowl, based on its unique painted design.

An archaeologist glues broken ceramic pieces from a typology pile into an entire object.

Chinese plate artifact

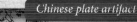

GREAT ZIMBABWE
Zimbabwe – Africa
c. 1000 – 1500 CE (500 – 1000 BP)

Just outside of these impressive stone walls were gold mines. What did the <u>Shona ancestors</u> in Great Zimbabwe society use that gold for?

To answer this question, archaeologists studied the typology of found artifacts. They noticed that beads, bracelets, glass, and pottery weren't African-style, but rather Chinese, Indian, and Middle Eastern. To acquire these fine items, Great Zimbabwe Shona ancestors must have traded their gold overseas!

Get It Down To A Science

Archaeologists use science and technology to discover what they can't see with the naked eye!

<u>**X-ray fluorescence (XRF)**</u> technology shows what artifacts are uniquely made of. XRF matches chemical compounds found in these artifacts, with rocks, metals, and clays from around the world. These results help archaeologists figure out where the artifacts were created.

element	conc. %
Silver (Ag)	0.00
Gold (Au)	0.00
Copper (Cu)	0.00
Iron (Fe)	0.00
Zinc (Zn)	0.00
Mercury (Hg)	0.00
Lead (Pb)	0.00
Tin (Sn)	100.00

video image: 320 x 240 pixels

<u>**CT scans**</u> take x-ray images of human and animal bodies, which archaeologists use to study bones and organs.

An XRF machine shows that this part of an ancient coin is made entirely out of tin!

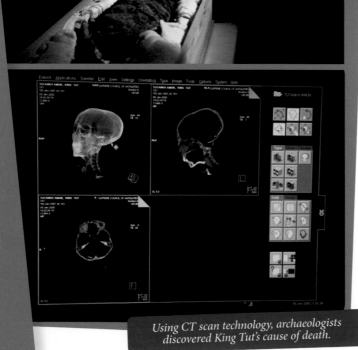

Using CT scan technology, archaeologists discovered King Tut's cause of death.

KING TUT'S TOMB

Words to Remember

<u>**Mummification**</u>: a way to preserve a dead human body over a long period of time by treating it with resins and salts and wrapping it up in cloth strips, commonly done in ancient Egypt

KING TUT FAMILY TREE

Archaeologists used DNA analysis to create King Tut's family tree.

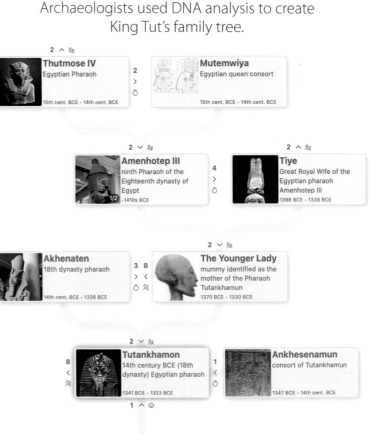

Thutmose IV
Egyptian Pharaoh
15th cent. BCE - 14th cent. BCE

Mutemwiya
Egyptian queen consort
15th cent. BCE - 14th cent. BCE

Amenhotep III
ninth Pharaoh of the Eighteenth dynasty of Egypt
-1410s BCE

Tiye
Great Royal Wife of the Egyptian pharaoh Amenhotep III
1398 BCE - 1338 BCE

Akhenaten
18th dynasty pharaoh
14th cent. BCE - 1336 BCE

The Younger Lady
mummy identified as the mother of the Pharaoh Tutankhamun
1370 BCE - 1330 BCE

Tutankhamon
14th century BCE (18th dynasty) Egyptian pharaoh
1341 BCE - 1323 BCE

Ankhesenamun
consort of Tutankhamun
1347 BCE - 14th cent. BCE

317a and 317b mummies
Daughters of Tutankhamun

Isotope analysis shows what human and animal bones are made of, so archaeologists can figure out what humans and animals ate during their lifetimes.

Testing this human skeleton from Rome using isotope analysis, we know this person ate tuna.

DNA analysis

helps archaeologists understand how humans, animals, or plants are connected and change over time.

KING TUT'S TOMB
Egypt - Africa
c. 1325 BCE (3325 BP)

Have you ever wanted to uncover a secret Egyptian royal tomb? Archaeologist Howard Carter did in 1922, and what he found inside was King Tutankhamun's (Tut's) mummy.

In ancient Egyptian **mummification**, priests did the following:
1. Removed all important human organs and put them in jars.
2. Cleaned the body and put a sticky goo called resin and salts on it.
3. Wrapped the body up in strips of cloth, placing small Egyptian god and animal figurines called amulets in between. These amulets were meant to protect King Tut in the afterlife.

CT scanning Tut's mummy, archaeologists discovered why he might have died at 19 years old. The young king had bone disease, and a broken leg which led to an infection. He also had signs of malarial disease in his brain.

Similar DNA results from both King Tut and mummies in other tombs help archaeologists figure out who was related in the Egyptian royal family tree!

33

KING TUT'S TOMB
GOLDEN TREASURE CHAMBERS

Archaeologists found over 5,000 objects in King Tut's tomb! Here are just a few:

- Wine jars, baskets of fruit, meat, and bread

- Beds and chairs

- Underwear, gloves, sandals, jewelry, makeup, and shaving tools

- 4 golden chariots

- Model boats and Egyptian games

- Writing tools

- Weapons and shields

- Statues of Tut and Egyptian gods

- A golden throne

According to ancient Egyptian beliefs, King Tut needed objects to bring with him into the afterlife: food, clothes, and other everyday items. He required these and all the golden riches to enjoy on his journey in the afterlife, just like the lavish royal life he had while living.

Dating...Not the Kind You Think

How do archaeologists know how old things are? They use relative and absolute dating. **Relative dating** is the process of comparing artifacts with one another to estimate their ages, like being older or more recent. **Absolute dating** is the process of scientifically measuring an artifact's actual age or age range.

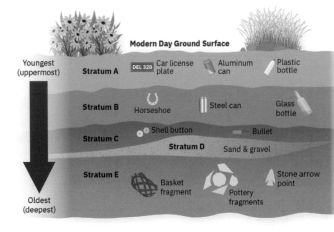

Relative Dating Methods

Stratigraphy

Artifacts in higher-up layers are more recent and artifacts in lower layers are older.

Typology

Artifacts that look similar were most likely created around the same time.

Absolute Dating Methods

Radiocarbon dating

Carbon in living things breaks down over time, which allow archaeologists to calculate the ages of these things.

Dendrochronology

Trees form circular ring patterns every year, which allow archaeologists to calculate the ages of wooden artifacts.

Uranium-series dating (U-series dating)

Similar to radiocarbon dating, uranium breaks down over time, which allow archaeologists to calculate the ages of rocks and bones.

L'ANSE AUX MEADOWS

Words to Remember

Viking: describing a group of travelers during the c. 700s - 1000s CE who came from Denmark, Norway, or Sweden

SULAWESI CAVE PAINTINGS

Words to Remember

Pre-Austronesian people: ancestors of the hundreds of millions of people in Asia and Australia around the world today

Warty pig: a pig with little hairs, from Sulawesi (doesn't actually have warts!)

L'ANSE AUX MEADOWS
Newfoundland, Canada - North America
c. 1000 CE (1000 BP)

During excavation, archaeologists found wood and charcoal ecofacts, and a bronze pin artifact. Archaeologists took these objects back to the lab for analysis and discovered the following:

1. The typology of the bronze pin is <u>Viking</u>-style.
2. The radiocarbon dating of the charcoal and dendrochronology of the wood calculated an age of 1,000 years old.

Putting these two findings together, they learned that Vikings were in North America around 1000 CE. This date is long before Christopher Columbus, previously thought to be the first European to sail to North America in 1492 CE!

Viking-style bronze pin

Archaeologists used three types of dating at L'Anse aux Meadows: typology, radiocarbon dating, and dendrochronology.

SULAWESI CAVE PAINTINGS
Island in Indonesia - Asia
c. 43500 - 18000 BCE (20000 - 45500 BP)

We have been drawing animals for 45,500 years! Using U-series dating, archaeologists tested paint that ancient <u>Pre-Austronesian people</u> used to create <u>warty pig</u> paintings on cave walls. The results proved that these are the oldest wall paintings in the world!

Before this discovery, the oldest cave art found was in Europe. The Sulawesi cave paintings shifted the focus of the origin of art from Europe to other parts of the world.

Using all the gathered evidence collected in the lab and at a site, an archaeologist detective tells stories to connect artifact clues to how people lived. This is called **interpretation**. There is no singular correct answer about the past—instead, there are many *possible* explanations. Let's interpret two groundbreaking sites together...

Ask Questions

Solve the case *Tell the possible stories*

SCAN FOR VIDEO

GÖBEKLI TEPE

Words to Remember

Neolithic period: a time frame when people started to stay in one place to farm, instead of just hunt and find food as they traveled

GÖBEKLI TEPE
Turkey – Middle East
c. 10000 – 8000 BCE (10000 – 12000 BP)

Skulls, scorpions, and feasts...all these things make up a possible story of Göbekli Tepe. During the early <u>Neolithic period</u>, people traveled here. Why?

Let's examine some archaeological clues: pillars in circles with animal carvings, animal bones, skulls with holes in them, and statues.

Vulture stone carving

What do the animal carvings mean? Why are there animal bones?

The carvings show animals as scary creatures, such as lions baring their sharp teeth and scorpions preparing to sting. Art found in caves elsewhere depict happy, frolicking animals. So, people at Göbekli Tepe may have believed animals were dangerous. Archaeologists also believe that found bones were left over from grand feasts.

What do the pillars mean?

They were built for a reason, likely as an important place for people to gather. Think of where you have seen pillars in your life, like religious places and town halls.

What do the skulls and head-themed statues mean?

The people making the statues and cuts in the skulls did it for a reason. We aren't sure why, but one theory is that there was a skull cult. This idea suggests people made cuts as part of their beliefs or religion.

So, an overall *possible interpretation* is that Göbekli Tepe was a special place for people to meet up and practice their beliefs, like an ancient temple.

UR
Words to Remember

Sumerian culture: one of the earliest groups of people who built cities in what is known as Mesopotamia (which includes today's Iraq)

Ziggurat: a pyramid-like building that had a temple at the top

Sacrifices: the acts of killing animals or people for religious or important purposes

Nanna: the Ur god of the Moon

SCAN FOR VIDEO

UR
Iraq – Middle East
c. 3000 – 1950 BCE (3950 – 5000 BP)

The city of Ur was a hub of <u>Sumerian culture</u>. It had everything from a huge <u>ziggurat</u> to a bustling town to an ancient cemetery full of amazing objects!

Let's learn about the people who lived there through these archaeological clues: royal graves like Queen Puabi's tomb, bodies in the Death Pit, a box called the Standard of Ur, and the ziggurat.

Queen's lyre from the Royal Cemetery

Royal Game of Ur (visit page 91 for more)

Why were people buried near the Royal Cemetery, some in the Death Pit?

The Sumerians believed in the afterlife and had special ways of taking care of the dead. The people in the Death Pit were likely **sacrifices**, killed for the recently buried king or queen.

What does Queen Puabi's tomb tell us?

She was a very rich person, and wanted to show it. Puabi wore expensive jewelry and a headdress, and was buried with extravagant objects and many servants. These servants would work for her in the afterlife.

What is shown on the Standard of Ur and what does it mean?

One side shows the king ordering soldiers into war. The other side shows the king supervising a sacrifice and feast. So, the Standard shows how powerful the king of Ur must have been in his multiple jobs: military leader, priest, and ruler.

What was the ziggurat used for?

The people at Ur believed in a Moon god named **Nanna**. At the top of the ziggurat once stood a temple, where the king and priests would bring gifts to Nanna to keep him happy. If the god was happy, then he would keep the city safe. If the city was safe, then the townspeople would be happy with the king.

So, an overall *possible interpretation* is that Ur royalty were rich and had a lot of power, everyday people following them in religious beliefs, peace, war, and death.

When interpreting archaeological sites, a singular site may not have all the answers. This is why archaeologists sometimes **compare** and **contrast** different sites from similar times and places.

STONEHENGE
England - Europe
c. 2800 - 1100 BCE (3100 - 4800 BP)

TRILITHON

STONE

STONEHENGE AND WOODHENGE
Words to Remember

European Neolithic period: a time frame of early farmers in Europe, after the Neolithic period in the Middle East

Henges: monument structures made out of stone or wood placed in circles

Trilithons: stacks of two stones with one stone laid out on top

HOW ARE THEY SIMILAR?
1) BOTH are from the **European Neolithic period** and located near one another.
2) BOTH are **henges** of the same size.
3) BOTH face the sunrise in the middle of Summer.

HOW ARE THEY DIFFERENT?
1) STONEHENGE is made of stone, while WOODHENGE is made of wood.
2) There are many henges like WOODHENGE, but just one STONEHENGE.
3) STONEHENGE has **trilithons**, while WOODHENGE does not.

So, what can archaeologists interpret by comparing and contrasting Stonehenge and Woodhenge?

WOODHENGE
England - Europe
c. 2500 - 1800 BCE (3800 - 4500 BP)

WOOD

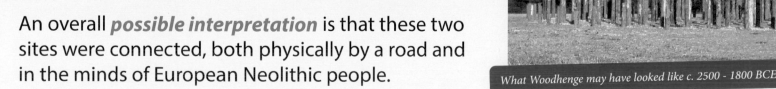

What Woodhenge may have looked like c. 2500 - 1800 BCE

An overall *possible interpretation* is that these two sites were connected, both physically by a road and in the minds of European Neolithic people.

The reason one is made of stone and the other is made of wood relates to these people's beliefs. Stone is connected with the dead, while wood is connected with the living. In this case, Stonehenge was built out of sturdy stone to last throughout the infinite afterlife, compared to the temporary wooden henges made for limited lifetimes.

STONEHENGE
SECRET OF THE STONES

For centuries, people have been asking about the secret meaning behind these stones. One interpretation we discussed is that Stonehenge is a place to celebrate the dead. Here are some other interesting theories as to why it exists:

- Druids, a priestly group, held meetings here.

- Irish giants built it, and Merlin the Magician was able to use his powers to zap the giants away (according to Geoffrey of Monmouth's book in 1136 CE).

- People performed human or animal sacrifices at the stones, killing for a spiritual reason.

- Ancient astronomers built it to track seasonal solstices and predict eclipses.

5 KEEP THE PAST ALIVE: WHAT HAPPENS NEXT?

Archaeologists find, excavate, clean, scientifically study, and interpret the artifacts. *Then what?* From there, some artifacts are kept safe in dry storage rooms. Notes and photographs are organized in shelved folders or on computer databases. Future archaeologists can visit these storage rooms to study objects again with newer technology, and people like you and I can go and view these cool artifacts!

Ancient Greek jars called amphoras displayed on storage shelves

Restoration and Reconstruction

Unlike smaller artifacts, larger features cannot be safely stored away from destructive rain and wind. Restoration and reconstruction preserve and rebuild important archaeological sites.

Restoration is work done to a site to repair damage caused by age and weather. The goal is make the site look as much as possible like it did *when it was first dug up*.

Reconstruction is work done to a site to make it look like it did *in the past when it was created*.

Visitors to these places today physically can step back in time to imagine what life may have been like back then!

Before and after reconstruction of the ziggurat ut Ur in Iraq

New computer technology can digitally reconstruct what the past may have looked like:

Temple of Vesta in Rome, Italy

Sanctuary of Fortuna Primigenia in Palestrina, Italy

Giza Pyramids in Egypt digital reconstruction

Museums and Artifact Ownership

Artifacts may be given to cultural groups whose ancestors made them, or to museums.

Museums are great places for us to learn about the past by looking at artifacts up close and in person. **Curators** are the people who carefully select, manage, and take care of these artifacts, sharing fascinating archaeological interpretations with visitors.

Asian Civilisations Museum in Singapore

Smithsonian National Museum of African American History and Culture in Washington, DC

BENIN BRONZES

Words to Remember

Kingdom of Benin: an empire that lasted from c. 1100 - 1900 CE in today's Southern Nigeria

Edo people: a group of around three million people who live today in Southern Nigeria, whose ancestors were part of the Benin Kingdom

Do all artifacts on display at museums belong there?

Many artifacts in European and American museums were taken from their home countries without permission. These artifacts are important to cultural groups to better understand and honor their pasts. The Benin Bronzes is one example among many...

Benin City, Nigeria

The Benin Bronzes (c. 1500 - 1900 CE, from Nigeria)

In the late 1800s, British soldiers took over 1,000 artifacts known as the Benin Bronzes from the **Kingdom of Benin** (Southwestern Nigeria today). They were placed In museums all over Europe and the United States. Since the 1960s, the **Edo people** have been asking for the artifacts to be returned to Nigeria, which would help restore an important piece of their history.

The British Museum (London, England) decided not to give up most of their 700 Benin Bronzes, and those they did return cost Nigeria a lot of money. Other museums like the Smithsonian National Museum of African Art (Washington, DC, USA) and the Ethnological Museum of Berlin (Germany) have decided to return their Bronzes. Nigeria plans to display the returned Benin Bronzes in a museum of their own.

Benin Bronzes on wall at the British Museum

A Benin Bronze at the British Museum

When visiting a museum, notice the information cards beside the artifacts. What do curators tell us about each artifact?

How it Got There
Not all artifacts were taken without permission. Cards may say if museums borrowed or purchased the artifact.

What, Where, and When
What it is made out of
Where in the world and which culture it came from
When the artifact was made

The Artifact's Story
The archaeologist's interpretation teaches us about how these museum artifacts are important to past cultures.

How do old artifacts survive the test of time to be able to be put on display in museums? Let's explore...

LOST AND FOUND:
WEATHER, NATURE, AND EROSION

Not everything from the past survives for archaeologists to one day dig up. **Organic** artifacts are made out of living things and can disappear! They vanish through **decomposition** or the process of things slowly breaking down until they become part of nature in the earth. For example, we know humans have always needed to eat to survive, yet archaeologists rarely find remains of ancient food at a dig site.

Weather and natural disasters like earthquakes and hurricanes can damage even the strongest structures.

Earthquakes in 2016 damaged the 600-year-old Kumamoto Castle in Japan.

Cyclone storm Giovanna damaged the 400-year-old Ambohimanga courtyard on the African island of Madagascar.

LAKE MUNGO

Words to Remember

Australian Aboriginal people: groups of people from Australia who came from Africa long ago

Weather and natural disasters aren't the only culprits: humans also damage artifacts and archaeological sites. Ancient Egyptian grave robbers stole gold artifacts from royal tombs, and humans today draw graffiti on the Sulawesi cave paintings.

Drought is a long period of time with very little rain, causing water to dry up. This condition—while threatening human survival—can reveal artifacts previously hidden under shallow bodies of water.

Like drought, erosion can be good and bad. **Erosion** is when weather or natural elements like wind or water push away sand or wear away parts of rocks over time.

Erosion can be **harmful** to archaeology because it slowly removes layers of rocky old things. This makes old structures look different than when they were first built.

Erosion can be **helpful** to archaeology when, over time, it reveals artifacts hidden underneath layers of sand or dirt.

Part of the Mungo Man's skull

LAKE MUNGO SKELETONS
New South Wales - Australia
c. 40000 BCE (42000 BP)

Long ago, Lake Mungo used to be...well...a lake. Now, it's a dried-up area, winds blowing up the sand causing lots of erosion. That's how two skeletons were slowly unearthed, spotted 42,000 years after they were buried!

These skeletons are called the Mungo Man and Lady, the oldest human remains found in Australia. Using DNA analysis, archaeologists determined that these two are related to today's <u>Australian Aboriginal people</u>. Since then, the Mungo Man and Lady have been returned to the Aboriginal people.

...dry desert...

...wet

FAYUM MUMMY PORTRAITS
Egypt - Africa
c. 100 BCE - 300 CE (1700 - 2100 BP)

Wood normally decomposes over time, but the dry Egyptian desert preserves organic artifacts. These portraits painted on wood were placed on top of mummies during burial. They show the hairstyle, jewelry, and clothing that people wore when Romans ruled over Egypt, long after the time of the Egyptian kings like Tut.

BOG BUTTER
Ireland and Scotland - Europe
Earliest c. 1000 BCE (3000 BP)

While normal butter decomposes quickly, Bog Butter—a fatty food like dairy—is preserved in a __bog__. Found in Ireland and Scotland, archaeologists believe this is how people stored food to keep it fresh before refrigerators.

11

bog...

...frozen land...

BOG BUTTER

Words to Remember

Bog: wet, muddy ground like a swamp

ÖTZI THE ICEMAN
Italy – Europe
c. 3350 – 3105 BCE (5105 – 5350 BP)

Frozen in the extreme cold of the Ötztal Alps, this man was found when ice surrounding him melted. Also preserved was the clothing he wore, which would normally decompose.

Ötzi the Iceman likely died from the arrowhead found in his shoulder. Archaeologists study his body, tools, and clothes to better understand early humans.

A modern painting of Vesuvius' eruption in 79 CE

...heap of rocky ash!

Wealthy people's homes

POMPEII
Italy – Europe
c. 600 BCE – 79 CE (1921 – 2600 BP)

Rumble. <u>Ancient Romans</u> screamed, running away from a horrifying sight: a huge volcanic eruption, spewing ash and <u>pyroclastic flow</u>. This volcano named Mount Vesuvius erupted in 79 CE, covering the city of Pompeii in layers of ash.

Because of this eruption, the hardened ash preserved the whole city as it was in 79 CE! Frozen in time were things that would otherwise fall apart or decompose: houses with beautiful wall paintings, restaurants (one with a loaf of bread still in the oven!), streets, bath houses, toilets, an amphitheater and theater, and the victims who could not escape...

POMPEII
Words to Remember

Ancient Romans: people who lived in Italy and around the Mediterranean, c. 750 BCE - 475 CE

Pyroclastic flow: an extremely hot volcanic mix of rock, ash, and gas

Casting: a method of preserving the shapes of bodies by filling air pockets in the earth with plaster

Restaurant and preserved bread

Plaster cast of a child

Plaster cast of a dog

Plaster cast of an adult

Plaster casts of a group of victims

POMPEII
PLASTER CAST ARCHAEOLOGY

The bodies of those who didn't escape and died at Pompeii were buried in layers of ash. Because of the special volcanic conditions, the ash hardened in place after the bodies decomposed, leaving only their bones.

<u>Casting</u> is filling these air pockets in the ash with plaster. Digging around the hardened plaster, archaeologists can remove the ash to see the casts of people or animals who died during the eruption of Mount Vesuvius.

CT scans of human casts show their clothing and dying positions. Detecting the teeth of each skeleton through the plaster, archaeologists know that people at Pompeii had healthy chompers.

Check out how cool these casts are!

STORIES UNTOLD:
HOUSEHOLD ARCHAEOLOGY

Since many organic things decompose over time, the things that best survive are sturdy features. These are structures like religious temples, Medieval castles, and funerary tombs. The people who made these were rulers, who had the riches to buy strong building materials and the power to gather less wealthy people to do the construction.

When archaeologists excavate a site, they usually find the structures and artifacts left behind by the rich and powerful, rather than those by more ordinary people in society like you and me. What about these neglected buildings and artifacts? Over the past few years, some archaeologists have focused on the lives of everyday people in ancient societies by locating and excavating smaller homes in these old cities. This is called **household archaeology**.

SCAN FOR VIDEO

TEOTIHUACÁN
Mexico - North America
c. 200 BCE - 750 CE (1250 - 2200 BP)

Teotihuacán is known for its grand pyramids and temples—The Pyramid of the Sun and The Pyramid of the Moon. Archaeologists have studied these for centuries. More recently, they began household archaeology projects.

During excavation, archaeologists uncovered walls that reminded them of apartment buildings. They interpreted that each family had a cluster of rooms as their home. Some families even buried their deceased relatives beneath their floors to remember and honor them.

COPÁN
Words to Remember

Mayans: groups of people from Mesoamerica (Mexico and Central America)

Hieroglyphs: symbols that mean something, like our ABCs

KNOSSOS
Words to Remember

Ancient Greek: describing people living in today's Greece and around the Mediterranean from c. 1100 BCE - 600 CE, who spoke the same Greek language and worshipped the same gods

Minotaur: a half-man, half-bull monster in ancient Greek mythology

Rhyton: a cup that looks like a bull horn

Fresco: a wall painting on wet plaster

Minoans: a cultural group of people from the area including Crete, c. 3500 - 1100 BCE

Artifacts can't speak for themselves, but people can. **History** is the study of past people using writing that they left behind. At sites where ancient societies had writing systems, what people wrote can help archaeologists interpret found artifacts more accurately.

Historians...   Archaeologists...

...study writing...   ...study artifacts...

...to understand how past people lived.

...to understand how American colonists thought about freedom.

Historians study the written Declaration of Independence....

Archaeologists study a tea chest artifact tossed overboard during the Boston Tea Party...

Deciphering ancient written languages can suddenly give a voice to a whole culture, unlocking how people in an ancient civilization thought. For example, archaeologists found and deciphered hieroglyphs at Copán (top right).

Ancient writing can be tricky to interpret. Individuals can have unique thoughts and opinions, creating stories from their own points of view. So, we have to be careful—the writing of one ancient person may not be how all ancient people thought.

COPÁN
Honduras – Central America
c. 100 – 900 CE (1100 – 1900 BP)

At the city of Copán near Tikal, the ancient **Mayans** climbed a grand staircase to a temple. On the sides of the staircase, archaeologists found over 2,500 **hieroglyphs**!

Through hard work, translators were able to decipher these symbols and determine what the staircase writing meant. It is the history of rulers in Copán which helped archaeologists interpret other artifacts found at the site.

throne room

Bull-leaping fresco

Bull rhyton

KNOSSOS
Island of Crete, Greece – Europe
c. 3000 – 1300 BCE (3300 – 5000 BP)

Ancient Greek storytellers wrote tales about a maze created by King Minos, thought to have ruled Knossos in the ancient past. At the center of that maze lived the **Minotaur**: a half-man, half-bull monster.

At the Knossos palace, archaeologists found a bull **rhyton** and a bull-leaping **fresco**. These artifacts tell a different story from the ancient Greeks'. The fresco shows **Minoans** at Knossos leaping over bulls as part of an athletic performance. In both artifacts, the bulls are shown as powerful and respected.

Archaeology reveals that the Minoans admired bulls and were peaceful people. These ancient stories about Minos and the Minotaur were likely how the ancient Greeks thought about Minoans, rather than how Minoans actually lived.

61

Digital reconstruction

KNOSSOS
AN A-MAZE-ING PALACE

Ancient Greek storytellers were not too far off when they called this place a maze. The Knossos palace had over 1,300 interconnected rooms!

The palace was built, destroyed by fires and earthquakes, and rebuilt three separate times. Each time the palace was renovated, it grew in size and beauty to become this winding maze!

But instead of a monstrous Minotaur at the center of the palace, there was a bull-leaping performance courtyard.

Thanks to Knossos restoration efforts, we can see how vibrant this colorful palace once was!

ART LEFT BEHIND:
ARCHAEOLOGY AND ART HISTORY

Like we do with writing, we express our thoughts and feelings through art. **Art history** is the study of art over time. Archaeologists often uncover crafted objects or paintings during excavation and when interpreting a finding, both archaeologists and art historians ask questions. *What do I see and what does it mean? What does it say about the people living at that time and place?*

Let's explore three examples of art at archaeological sites: wall paintings, stone carvings, and statues.

ANAK TOMB
Words to Remember

Goguryeo: a kingdom in Northern Korea and Southern China from c. 0 - 700 CE

Guiyi: layers of cloth with ribbons hanging down, worn by important Chinese women for fancy occasions

ANAK TOMB NO. 3 WALL PAINTINGS
North Korea – Asia
c. 357 CE (1643 BP)

Archaeologists and art historians look at these paintings to learn how the <u>Goguryeo</u> people lived. Both interpret that the married man and woman in the paintings (above) were rich and powerful. The man is draped in expensive red silk and his wife wears a <u>guiyi</u>. These two had a lot of money to dress well in their lives. In the painting depicting a crowd (top left), the man is pulled in a cart, putting him at the center of the show.

Archaeologists and art historians can also learn what everyday life was like for the married couple's helpers. The people shown in the kitchen (bottom left) are cooking, taking care of animals, and helping the family in the home.

BAYON TEMPLE
Words to Remember

Khmer culture: an empire that had the capital city Angkor c. 800 - 1400 CE

Buddha: a teacher of Buddhism, who is worshipped in this religion

Guise: a likeness; like disguise; a way to look like someone else

BAYON TEMPLE STONE CARVINGS
Angkor Thom, Cambodia - Asia
c. 1100 - 1350 CE (650 - 900 BP)

In the middle of the jungle lies the capital city of the **Khmer culture**, Angkor. King Jayavarman VII built the Bayon Temple here, a religious place to worship **Buddha**.

Archaeologists and art historians interpret that these smiling faces (top) are King Jayavarman VII in the **guise** of Buddha. The king had these faces made to display his religious power.

His military power is depicted in the carving of the king riding an elephant into battle (middle). We can learn how everyday Khmer people lived through the images of them cooking rice and trading goods (bottom).

65

TERRACOTTA ARMY

Words to Remember

Mausoleum: a monumental space for a ruler or person of high status who died

Qin Dynasty: the first empire of China created by Qin Shi Huang, that lasted from c. 221 - 206 BCE

Terracotta: cooked clay

Restoration of statues in full color

Horses and chariot

SCAN FOR VIDEO

TERRACOTTA ARMY
Qin Shi Hyang's Mausoleum
Xi'an, China – Asia
c. 250 – 200 BCE (2200 – 2250 BP)

Qin Shi Huang, the first ruler of China, had his <u>mausoleum</u> built during the <u>Qin Dynasty</u>. Inside are over 8,000 <u>terracotta</u> warrior statues.

Each statue is life-sized and as heavy as a gorilla! 3D digital models of these statues show that each warrior has unique facial features, ears, and hairstyle.

Using technology, archaeologists discovered that the statues were once very bright in color and certain colors showed their army rank.

Why did Qin Shi Huang have a whole Terracotta Army buried with him? Archaeologists and art historians interpret that Qin Shi Huang wanted this army for protection in the afterlife against angry enemies he had killed in war.

Close-up of the unique faces

67

Archaeologists can specialize in different studies, such as becoming an expert on certain artifacts, or digging in certain places in the world.

Zooarchaeologists are archaeologists who study animal bones.

A Scythian carpet showing horse riding

PAZYRYK HORSE BURIALS

Words to Remember

Scythian: describing people living from c. 700 - 300 BCE in today's Ukraine, Kazakhstan, and Southern Russia

ANCIENT DELPHI

Words to Remember

Oracle: someone who predicts the future or voices advice from a god

Apollo: the ancient Greek god of archery, music, medicine, and prediction

Pythia: Apollo's oracle

Pythian games: a sporting event that happened every four years at Delphi, like today's Summer Olympics

Pentathlon: an ancient Greek sport including five events: sprinting, throwing a disc, throwing a pointed stick called a javelin, long jumping, and wrestling

PAZYRYK HORSE BURIALS
Siberia, Russia – Asia
c. 300 BCE (2300 BP)

Burying horses with someone who passed away was part of **Scythian** tradition. Digging in the Pazyryk Valley, zooarchaeologists noticed the skeletons of horses decorated with saddles alongside people in tombs.

Zooarchaeologists interpret that the Pazyryk Scythians believed that horses were important. The Scythian people not only rode and traded horses, but chose to dress them up in saddles and sacrifice them in honoring human burials.

Archaeobotanists are archaeologists who study plants.

Classical archaeologists are archaeologists who study things in the Mediterranean region of Europe.

Archaeobotanists study crops like wheat to understand what people planted and ate.

Left: Statue of Apollo
Right: Painting of the Pythia

ANCIENT DELPHI
Greece – Europe
c. 1500 – 300 BCE (2300 – 3500 BP)

For ancient Greeks who wanted to watch sports or know their futures, Delphi was the place to be! Known as the belly-button of the ancient Greek world, classical archaeologists study this site to learn about the <u>oracle</u> of <u>Apollo</u> (called the <u>Pythia</u>) and the <u>Pythian Games</u>.

People visited a special temple to ask the Pythia questions. The Pythia passed along Apollo's advice or future predictions to them.

The exciting Pythian Games drew ancient Greek people from far and wide...

ANCIENT DELPHI PYTHIAN GAMES

Bronze statue of a charioteer

Stadium for sporting events

Similar to today's Summer Olympic Games, the Pythian Games happened every four years. Sports at this five-day event took place in the stadium and gymnasium and included wrestling, boxing, running, chariot racing, and the pentathlon. The <u>pentathlon</u> spectacular had five events: sprinting, hurling a heavy disc, throwing a pointed stick called a javelin, long jumping, and wrestling.

Because the Pythian Games were for Apollo who is also the god of the arts, there were other competitions in addition to sports. These were special contests held in the theater (left) including plays, speeches, poetry, and musical instruments.

Which sporting or artistic event do you imagine yourself winning at ancient Delphi?

EASTER ISLAND

Words to Remember

Moai: giant stone statues with faces carved into them

Rapa Nui people: those whose ancestors came to Easter Island from Polynesia (a group of islands off the Australian coast)

EASTER ISLAND MOAI
Easter Island, territory of Chile – South America
c. 1000 – 1680 CE (320 –1000 BP)

This island is not named after the bunny and egg hunt holiday. Rather, it is famous for the <u>moai</u> heads.

Each moai head statue weighs as much as a blue whale! How did the <u>Rapa Nui people</u> move them from the island's volcano to its shores?

Experimental archaeologists put this question to the test by sliding the heads on water and juice, rolling them on wood, and even walking the statues with ropes (right).

Experimental archaeologists are archaeologists who make replicas of old artifacts to test out theories about how they worked and were used.

Paleoarchaeologists are archaeologists who study ancient human fossils.

A paleoarchaeologist excavates a human skeleton.

SCAN FOR VIDEO

Underwater archaeologists are archaeologists who study things that sank to the bottom of bodies of water.

A deep-sea vehicle called ALVIN sent down to explore the Titanic

The captain's bathroom

A passenger's watch stopped at 2:20am, the time of the sinking.

RMS TITANIC SHIPWRECK
Atlantic Ocean between Southampton, England and New York City, USA
April 15, 1912 CE (88 BP)

Not all archaeology takes place in ancient BCE or on land—some sites are more recent and underwater, like the Titanic.

On its very first voyage, the RMS Titanic struck an iceberg, sinking to the bottom of the ocean. The ship was called "unsinkable" because of its safety features, but the iceberg damage caused catastrophic flooding. Only around 710 of the 2,224 people aboard survived by escaping in lifeboats.

The RMS Titanic wreck was found in 1985 CE in the Atlantic Ocean, more than two miles underwater. Because of the depth and the high water pressure, human diving wasn't an option. Underwater archaeologists had to use technology to dive down to the ship. They sent deep-sea vehicles and attached robots to take photos, record videos, and collect artifacts. This technology allowed archaeologists to create 3D models of the ship, and study and restore thousands of objects left behind by the passengers.

73

SCAN FOR VIDEO

THE EASTER ISLAND MOAI ARE WATCHING

According to ancient Rapa Nui beliefs, their ancestors live inside these moai. When an important Rapa Nui person died, a moai statue would be built in their honor and ceremoniously moved to a stone platform.

Through carved eyes, ancestors watch over the island to protect the Rapa Nui people.

With around 1,000 moai on Easter Island, most lining the coast, the ancestors have eyes everywhere to keep the island and its inhabitants safe.

ARCHAEOLOGY AND YOU:
BECOME AN ARCHAEOLOGIST

Just as special types of archaeologists contributed to what we know about the past,

KIDS also contribute to archaeology!

Matthew Berger holding the found Australopithecus sediba (human fossil)

"Tau!" called **nine-year-old** Matthew Berger, as he ran after his dog through the grassland of Johannesburg, South Africa in 2008. While chasing after his pet, he tripped and fell over a log! When Matthew looked up, he came face-to-face with an important part of human history never before found.

Matthew had stumbled upon the bones of someone who lived around two million years ago, which is a HUGE archaeological discovery!

Archaeologists choose to do archaeology because they...

... love it!

... want to uncover mysteries of the past.

... like different types of learning, such as hands-on work excavating at a site and thinking about what artifacts mean.

... enjoy working with others who are also passionate about archaeology.

... value assisting cultures in rediscovering and understanding their pasts.

Some kids that contribute grow up to be professional archaeologists!

David Stuart studying Mayan hieroglyphs at Copán

When he was a kid in the 1970s, David Stuart became fascinated by the art and writing found at Mayan sites like Tikal and Copán. At **twelve years old**, he wrote an academic paper on deciphering these Mayan hieroglyphs. As a teenager, he assisted historians and archaeologists in translating hieroglyphs and was awarded a MacArthur Genius Grant for his passion in the field.

David Stuart loved studying Mayan art and writing so much that he decided to make a career out of it! Today, he is a professional archaeologist and professor.

You can take steps now to become an archaeologist one day! All you need is to be interested in archaeology, seek out more information, and try activities at home. When you become an adult, you can go to college to get a degree in archaeology!

Archaeology students and teachers posing for a photo after a long day of excavation at a site in Southwestern New Mexico, USA.

Where Do Archaeologists Work

EXCAVATION AND ARTIFACT CARE

Archaeological excavation field worker

Digs at archaeological sites

Cultural resource manager

Manages and protects important archaeological sites and artifacts belonging to cultural groups

National or local government or organization employee

Hired by their city, state, or country to do archaeology, such as working for the National Park Service

Lab technician & analyst

Develops and uses science technology to study archaeological artifacts (scientific dating, conservation techniques, X-ray fluorescence, DNA analysis)

Computer scientist

Compiles archaeological site data and makes 3D digital reconstructions of sites and artifacts

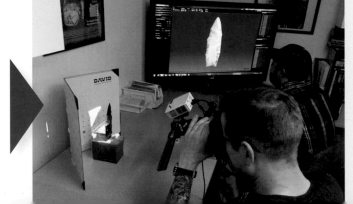

SCIENCE AND TECHNOLOGY

EDUCATION

Writer

Creates educational research or stories (fiction and nonfiction) based on archaeological evidence

Museum curator

Manages and takes care of artifacts in a museum

University or college professor

Teaches students about archaeology

Site tour guide

Educates tourists about certain archaeological sites

Movie, TV show, or video game consultant

Helps make stories for entertainment historically accurate

ENTERTAINMENT AND MEDIA

ARCHAEOLOGY IS A **BIG** DEAL!

Now you know what archaeology is and how it works, but why is it so important?

The Great Wall of China

Let's revisit what makes archaeology so *groundbreaking*...

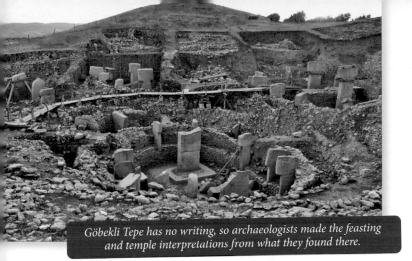

Göbekli Tepe has no writing, so archaeologists made the feasting and temple interpretations from what they found there.

THE MORE YOU KNOW

Humans have been leaving behind objects for around 200,000 years, but only learned how to write around 5,200 years ago. That is 194,800 years of NO written history, which is why we need archaeology to interpret objects.

HISTORY OFTEN REPEATS ITSELF

Archaeologists tell us stories about how people once lived, through artifacts. If we know the mistakes people made in the past, we are less likely to repeat them.

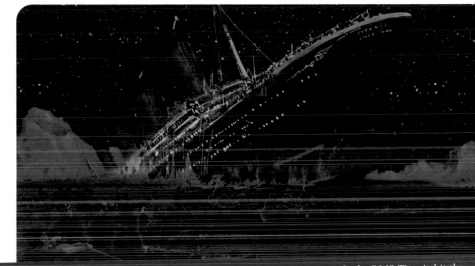

By studying the ship wreckage, underwater archaeologists determined how exactly the RMS Titanic hit the iceberg. Archaeological information on how the ship sank validates safety measures applied after the tragedy.

RESTORATION, RECONSTRUCTION, AND MUSEUMS

Archaeology keeps stories alive in museums, artifact storage rooms, and at restored sites so that visitors can experience what life may have been like long ago.

The Huchimalli Gudi temple restoration at Aihole, India shows us how it looked long ago.

Gallery with artifacts in the National Museum, New Delhi, India

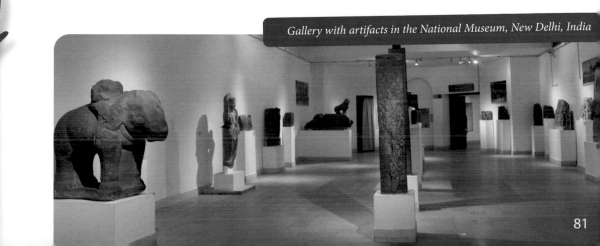

RESCUE ARCHAEOLOGY

Each year, countless old buildings are torn down to build new structures. But construction vehicles can demolish valuable artifacts in their paths. **Rescue archaeologists** are those who are called in to carefully dig up artifacts before construction. Since artifacts are stories about the human past, archaeologists help save history from being destroyed forever!

Rescue archaeologists in Bath, England search for artifacts before construction on the land.

HONORING ANCESTORS

Archaeologists tell the stories of people's ancestors, especially of native cultures around the world. With these told stories, each indigenous group can better preserve their cultural traditions, lifestyle, and history. This is known as **heritage**. Present-day cultural groups such as the Choctaw, Shona, Rapa Nui, and Aboriginal Australians celebrate their heritages.

The Choctaw ancestors built Cahokia.

The Shona ancestors traded gold at Great Zimbabwe.

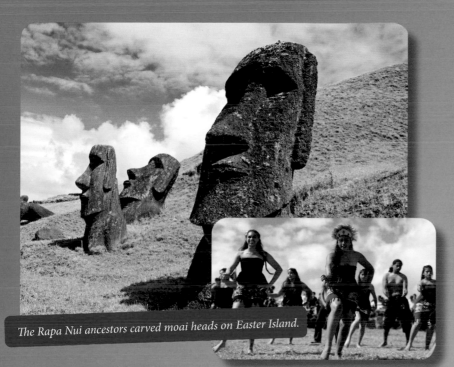

The Rapa Nui ancestors carved moai heads on Easter Island.

The Aboriginal ancestors fished at Lake Mungo.

CAN YOU DIG IT?

You've traveled around the world and through time in this book. Now you know many things about archaeology—*what it is*, *how it works*, and *where you find it!*

We only just scratched the surface of archaeology and there is still so much more to learn! Don't stop here. Keep *digging up* more information, just like a professional archaeologist would.

Be a detective and a storyteller! Ask questions loud and proud. Get your hands a little dirty. Think about what your discoveries are trying to tell you and what it all may mean. Then share your stories.

And most important, have fun, future archaeologists! *Dig it!*

Ancient home from Ephesus, Turkey.

Here are some archaeology activities to try at home or in the classroom (with your parent's, caregiver's, or teacher's permission):

Cleaning your Unit and the Munsell Chart

What you need: color printer, printer paper, computer, gardening trowel, large garden pot, dirt, camera

1. Visit **https://bit.ly/MunsellChart** or scan the QR code (left) and print out the Munsell Chart.
2. Pour dirt unevenly into a large garden pot, leaving a couple inches of room at the top.
3. Take a small amount of dirt and place it on the various Munsell Chart colors from the printed pages. Determine what color matches best.
4. Take your gardening trowel and using the edge, scrape against the dirt. Get the dirt as flat and even as possible.
5. From above, take a photo of your pot of dirt. *In archaeology, the pot of dirt represents a cleaned unit.*

Shaker Screen

What you need: kitchen colander with big holes, uncooked/dried rice, round fruit-flavored cereal, two bowls (one of them bigger than the colander), counter space

1. Pour 3-4 cups of uncooked/dried rice into the smaller bowl, then pour 1 cup of the cereal into that same bowl. Stir with your hands or a spoon until well mixed.
2. Place the bigger bowl underneath the colander on the kitchen counter. Pour the rice and cereal mixture into the colander. Slightly lift the colander and lightly shake it so that the smaller pieces of rice fall through the colander holes into the bigger bowl. The rice should separate into the bigger bowl with the cereal left in the colander. *In archaeology, the colander represents a shaker screen, used to separate the rice from the cereal (like a shaker screen separates the dirt from the artifacts).*

Typology

What you need: round fruit-flavored cereal, counter space

1. Using the cereal from the last activity, group the cereal pieces *(artifacts)* into a pile on the counter, based on color. This is their *typology*.
2. Eating the cereal is optional!

Household Archaeology and Interpretation

What you need: various random objects around your home

1. Take a slow walk around your home and notice all the objects, big and small.
2. Ask yourself questions about each of the objects:
   - *Why is this object important to my family?*
   - *What does it say about how I live each day?*
   - *How does it relate to my town or my country in the current year in which I am living?*

The Stratigraphy Cake

**What you need: boxed cake mix, frosting, and baking supplies
OR an already-baked layered cake, plastic knife**

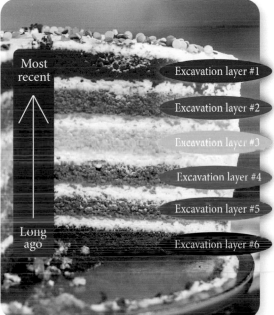

1. Go to the grocery store and get cake mix and frosting OR an already-baked layered cake (if you got an already-baked cake, skip to step #4).
2. Follow recipe instructions on the cake mix box to bake the layers of the cake with help from a parent, caregiver, or teacher. The layers will be the same color, but you can add food coloring to each layer to make it a rainbow cake (left).
3. Once the cake layers are baked and cooled, add frosting on top of each layer and stack the layers on top of one another, first layer on bottom and last layer on top.
4. With help from a parent, caregiver, or teacher, cut and remove a v-shaped slice of the cake to reveal the inside cake and frosting layers. *In archaeology, the cake layers represent the strata.*
5. Look at those cake *strata*! Each layer of cake and frosting are different. Which layers did you decorate first and last? The layers of frosting at the top are the most recent layers, just like in stratigraphy. Eating is optional!

Time Capsule: Leaving Artifacts for Future Archaeologists

**What you need: medium-sized see-through plastic box with sealable top,
objects of your own choosing, paper, pen**

A time capsule is a container of buried things from your life today, to be found by others in the future!

1. Gather objects that would help anyone who found your time capsule in the future better understand your life.

   Capsule Ideas: *magazine or newspaper with the current year; award ribbon, medal, or trophy; photo of you with your friends or family; written letter about yourself; USB drive with photos, videos, or your favorite songs*
2. Fill and seal your time capsule box. With permission from a parent, caregiver, or teacher, find a spot in the ground to bury your time capsule. Dig a hole with a shovel, place your time capsule inside the hole, and bury it.
3. Write a note that you buried a time capsule and when to dig it up. Keep the note or give it to someone to save. Now, you or others who read your note in the future can dig up your time capsule and learn about your life at the time you buried it!

Dress Like An Archaeologist

What do you have in your wardrobe to dress like an archaeologist?

Archaeology Site Digital Reconstructions

Visit this website or scan this QR code to watch sites transform into what they looked like in the ancient past:
https://bit.ly/DigitalReconstructions

US National Park Service Archaeology Booklet

Visit this website or scan this QR code to download this archaeology guide and activity booklet for kids:
https://bit.ly/NPSArchaeologyBooklet

Additional Archaeology Activities

Visit this website or scan this QR code to discover more archaeological activites for kids:
https://bit.ly/ArchaeologyActivities

Archaeology Talks and Classes

Be on the lookout for educational talks about archaeology at museums, universities, libraries, or community centers. Some of them are free and they are all great ways to learn more about archaeology and ask professionals questions.

Club and Organization Events

Some groups in your area may have digs or activities open to everyone! Even some scouting programs do excavations. Be sure to join in on the fun for some experience!

Summer Camps

Want to dig at a site? There are day- or week-long excavation camps! One example is at the Center for American Archeology (Kampsville, Illinois). With an adult, search the web on camps or programs near you to see what your area offers!

https://bit.ly/CenterforAmericanArcheology

Visit libraries to learn about sites like this one: The Library of Celsus (Roman building in Anatolia, which is the country of Turkey today).

Visit our **WunderMill Books YouTube channel** and **Persnickety Press Website** for more activities, tutorials, education guides, and information.

https://bit.ly/WunderMillYouTube

https://bit.ly/PersnicketyPress

Stardew Valley (PC and Mac, Xbox One, Playstation 4, Nintendo Switch, iOS and Android): Find artifacts and donate them to the museum or field office for fun rewards! You can visit the museum curator, Gunther, to donate artifacts, minerals, and lost books you find around your world. Dig up a chipped amphora (ancient vase), arrowhead, ancient doll, chewing stick (ancient toothbrush), ancient sword, ancient drum, golden mask, and ancient human bones!

To learn more about Stardew Valley, visit this website or scan the QR code: *https://bit.ly/StardewValleyGame*

Animal Crossing (Nintendo Switch, iOS and Android, Nintendo 3DS): Tell a story about your created world using artifacts! Blathers, a cute owl curator, is in charge of the natural history museum. Like an archaeologist, you can dig up things and give them to Blathers to build up your collection. Thanks to your donations, you can take your friends on a museum tour, showing them all the fossils you found!

To learn more about Animal Crossing, visit this website or scan the QR code: *https://bit.ly/AnimalCrossingGames*

Excavate! Games (Web browsers, iOS and Android): Uncover the famous ancient civilizations of Rome, Greece, Egypt, Mesoamerica, Mesopotamia, and the Byzantine Empire! Each with its own game, become an archaeologist by excavating and finding ancient artifacts that reveal amazing stories about the past. (Educators, each game includes a teacher's guide!)

To learn more about these six games, visit this website or scan the QR code: *https://bit.ly/DigItExcavateGames*

Copán: Mayan Hieroglyphs

What you need: computer, printer paper, printer, notebook paper, pencil

There are fantastic websites where you can learn how to write your name using the same Mayan hieroglyphs that were found at Copán! Visit this website for a print-out activity page or scan the QR code (it takes a moment to load): ***https://bit.ly/CopanMayanHieroglyphs***

Pompeii: Ancient Bread

What you need: recipe, tools and ingredients required in the recipe

Make bread like the Pompeiian baker, Numerius Popidius Priscus, who left his bread in the oven when Mount Vesuvius erupted! With help of a parent, caregiver, or teacher, try the recipe found on this website or scan the QR code: ***https://bit.ly/PompeiiAncientBread***

Ur: Game of Ur

What you need: computer

After studying the Game of Ur, found in the Royal Cemetery at Ur, archaeologists have figured out how to play this board game. Now you can play it, too! Visit this website or scan the QR code to see if you can win: ***https://bit.ly/GameofUr***

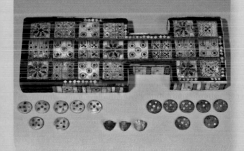

RMS Titanic: Rust Science Experiment

What you need: steel wool pad, 2 clear cups, water, vegetable oil

Over the past 100 years underwater, the Titanic has grown rusty. Rust formed on iron artifacts and the ship in a scientific chemical reaction between the iron and surrounding water. See how rust forms in water with this home science experiment found at this website or by scanning the QR code: ***https://bit.ly/TitanicRustExperiment***

Bayon Temple: The Art of Guise

What you need: drawing paper, pencil

We learned about King Jayavarman VII taking on the guise of Buddha at the Bayon Temple. Draw yourself in the guise of someone you admire. How can you make it look like yourself but also like that person, too? Make sure to include important attributes—things that help you recognize who is who—like objects either of you may love (examples: soccer ball, stuffed animal)!

GLOSSARY

- **Aboriginal Australian culture**: groups of people still thriving today in Australia who came from Africa around 50,000 years ago

- **Absolute Dating**: the process of scientifically measuring something's actual age or age range

- **Aerial photographs**: images from up high (like in a plane) of the ground below to see if it's a good place for an archaeological dig

- **Ancestors**: people who lived many years before you in your family or cultural group

- **Ancient**: long, long ago

- **Ancient Greek**: describing people living in today's Greece and around the Mediterranean from c. 1100 BCE - 600 CE, who spoke the same Greek language and worshipped the same gods

- **Ancient Romans**: people who lived in Italy and around the Mediterranean from c. 750 BCE - 475 CE, including Pompeii

- **Apollo**: the ancient Greek god of archery, music, medicine, and prediction

- **Archaeobotanists**: archaeologists who study plants

- **Archaeologists**: people who do archaeology

- **Archaeology**: "the study of ancient things"; a field asking questions about past humans, looking at dug-up things, figuring out answers to those questions, and telling the world those stories

- **Art history**: the study of art created over time

- **Artifacts**: objects made or used by humans in the past, dug up in archaeology

- **Backfilling**: to put dirt back in an already dug unit at an archaeological site

- **BCE (Before the Common Era)**: the time before CE began; the older or further back in time, the larger the date is

- **Bog**: wet, muddy ground like a swamp

- **BP**: "before present," meaning how many years ago from around the current time

- **Buddha**: a teacher of Buddhism, who is worshipped in this religion

- **c. (Circa)**: around the time of a certain date

- **Casting**: a method of preserving the shapes of bodies at Pompeii by filling air pockets in the earth with plaster

- **CE (Common Era)**: the time we've been in for the past 2,000+ years, we're in right now, and we'll be in tomorrow and into the future

- **Classical archaeologists**: archaeologists who study things in the Mediterranean region in Europe

- **CT scans**: x-rays that show bones and the body's tissues around the bones in 3D pictures

- **Culture**: a group of people who share parts of their lifestyle and traditions, which is how they define who they are

- **Curators**: the people who manage and take care of artifacts in a museum

- **Decomposition**: the process of slowly breaking down, so that thing becomes part of nature and disappears into the earth

- **Dendrochronology**: a type of absolute dating that measures tree ring patterns over time to calculate ages of wooden artifacts

- **Dig**: in archaeology, the careful excavation process at an archaeological site

- **DNA analysis**: studying the unique building blocks of living things to understand how humans, animals, and plants are connected and evolve over time

- **Drought**: a long period of time with very little rain, causing water to dry up, which could reveal artifacts

- **Ecofacts**: natural things left behind or used by humans

- **Edo people**: a group of around three million people who live today in Southern Nigeria, whose ancestors were part of the Benin Kingdom

- **Erosion**: when weather like wind or natural elements like flowing water push away sand or wear away parts of rocks over time

- **European Neolithic period**: the time frame from c. 7000 - 2000 BCE of early farmers in Europe, after the Neolithic period in the Middle East, including when Stonehenge and Woodhenge were built

- **Excavation**: the careful digging process at an archaeological site

- **Experimental archaeologists**: archaeologists who make replicas of old artifacts to test out theories about how artifacts worked

- **Features**: things built by humans that are too big to pack up and send back to the lab during a dig

- **Fresco**: painting originally done on wet plaster on a wall, such as the Bull-Leaping Fresco at Knossos

- **Geoglyphs**: "ground drawings," such as the Nazca Lines

- **Goguryeo**: a kingdom in Northern Korea and Southern China from c. 0 - 700 CE

- **Grid**: side by side square units that an archaeological site is divided into

- **Ground-penetrated radar (GPR)**: survey technology which sends an electric and magnetic shock into the ground

- **Guise**: a likeness; like a disguise; an attempt to look like someone else

- **Guiyi**: layers of cloth with ribbons hanging down, worn by important Chinese women for fancy occasions

- **Henges**: monument structures made out of stone or wood placed in circles

- **Heritage**: the traditions, lifestyle, and history of ancestors honored in a cultural group

- **Hieroglyphs**: symbols that mean something, like our ABCs

- **History**: the study of past people using writing they left behind

- **Household archaeology**: the study of things left behind by everyday people in a home, like at Teotihuacán

- **Inca Empire**: the kingdom of people (Inca) in Peru, Ecuador, Bolivia, Argentina, Chile, and Colombia from c. 1400s - 1500s CE, including Machu Picchu

- **Interpretation**: thinking hard to try to understand the meaning of something

- **Isotope Analysis**: looking at what types of elements on the periodic table things are made of to better understand those things

- **Khmer culture**: an empire that had the capital city Angkor c. 800 - 1400 CE where the Bayon Temple is

- **Kingdom of Benin**: an empire that lasted from c. 1100 - 1900 CE in today's Southern Nigeria, whose people created Benin Bronzes

- **LiDAR**: "light detection and ranging"; using an invisible laser to scan the ground to see if there is anything there to dig up in archaeology

- **Mausoleum**: a monumental space for a ruler or rich person who died, like Qin Shi Huang

- **Mayans**: cultural groups of people still thriving today from Mesoamerica (Mexico and Central America), like at Tikal and Copán

- **Minoans**: a cultural group of people from the area including Crete from c. 3500 - 1100 BCE

- **Minotaur**: a half-man, half-bull monster in ancient Greek mythology

- **Mississippian Native American**: describing cultural groups who lived near the Mississippi River from c. 1000 - 1500 CE

- **Moai**: giant stone statues with faces carved into them at Easter Island

- **Mound**: pyramid-like hill of dirt with a flat instead of pointed top, like at Cahokia

- **Mummification**: a way to preserve a dead human body by treating it with resins and salts and wrapping it up in cloth strips, commonly done for royalty in ancient Egypt

- **Munsell chart**: a guide that archaeologists use to help them record what color the soil is at an excavation site

- **Mythology**: stories to explain religion or culture, usually about the gods

- **Nanna**: the Ur god of the Moon

- **Neolithic period**: when people started to stay in one place to farm instead of just hunt and find food as they traveled

- **Oracle**: someone who predicts the future or voices advice from a god in ancient Greece

- **Organic**: made out of living things

- **Paleoarchaeologists**: archaeologists who study ancient human fossils

- **Pentathlon**: a sporting event in ancient Greek athletics including five events: sprinting, discus throw, javelin throw, long jump, and wrestling

- **Pre-Austronesian people**: ancestors of the hundreds of millions of people on Asia and Australia continents around the world today

- **Pyroclastic flow**: an extremely hot volcanic mix of rock, ash, and gas

- **Pythia**: Apollo's oracle at Ancient Delphi

- **Pythian games**: a sporting event that happened every four years in ancient Delphi, like today's Summer Olympics

- **Qin Dynasty**: the first empire of China created by Qin Shi Huang, that lasted from c. 221 - 206 BCE

- **Radiocarbon dating**: a type of absolute dating that measures how the element carbon breaks down over time in living things to calculate their ages

- **Rapa Nui people**: those still thriving today whose ancestors came from Polynesia (a group of islands off of Australia) to Easter Island

- **Reconstruction**: work done to a site to make it look like it did in the past when it was created

- **Relative dating**: the process of comparing artifacts with one another to estimate their ages, like being older or more recent

- **Rescue archaeologists**: archaeologists who study ancient things by saving them from being destroyed

- **Restoration**: work done to a site to repair damage caused by age and weather to make the site look similar to how it did when it was first dug up

- **Rhyton**: a cup that looks like a bull horn

- **Sacrifices**: the killings of animals or people for religious or important cultural purposes

- **Sample**: the method of digging at smaller part of a big site to try to understand the whole site

- **Scythian**: describing people living from c. 700 - 300 BCE in today's Ukraine, Kazakhstan, and Southern Russia

- **Shona**: one of the cultural groups who live in Zimbabwe today

- **Sites**: the lands where archaeologists excavate

- **Stratigraphy**: an archaeological concept that things that are older are buried at deeper layers in the ground

- **Stratum**: a layer of the earth that represents a time frame in stratigraphy

- **Sumerian culture**: one of the earliest groups of people from c. 4000 - 1500 BCE who built cities in what was known as Mesopotamia, like at Ur

- **Survey**: to inspect a possible site before deciding to dig there

- **Terracotta**: cooked clay

- **Texture**: how something feels, like the type of soil or dirt in an archaeological dig

- **Trilithons**: stacks of two stones with one stone laid out on top, found at Stonehenge

- **Typology**: the practice of grouping artifacts together in the lab based on how they look or what they are

- **Underwater archaeologists**: archaeologists who study things sunk in bodies of water

- **Unit**: the square section of dirt an archaeologist digs in at a site

- **Uranium-series dating (U-series dating)**: a type of absolute dating that measures how much the element uranium breaks down over time to calculate the ages of rocks and bones

- **Viking**: describing a group of travelers during the c. 700s - 1000s CE who came from from Denmark, Norway, or Sweden

- **Warty pig**: a pig with little hairs from Sulawesi (doesn't actually have warts!), drawn in early wall paintings in Indonesia

- **X-ray fluorescence (XRF)**: technology that tells us what chemical compounds artifacts are made of

- **Ziggurat**: a pyramid-like building that had a temple at the top, like at Ur

- **Zooarchaeologists**: archaeologists who study animals

BIBLIOGRAPHY

"Ancient Observatories - Timeless Knowledge." *Stanford University Solar Center,* http://solar-center.stanford.edu/AO/Ancient-Observatories.pdf.

"Angkor Thom, Cambodia: The Great Temple City." *Films On Demand,* Films Media Group, 1995, fod.infobase.com/PortalPlaylists.aspx?wID=102632&xtid=144262.

"Artifacts." *Stardew Valley Wiki,* 9 Jan. 2022, https://stardewvalleywiki.com/Artifacts.

Ballard, Robert D. *The Discovery of the* Titanic. Warner Books, 1995.

Battini, Laura. "Puabi." *The Encyclopedia of Ancient History,* 26 Oct. 2012, https://doi-org.libproxy.lib.unc.edu/10.1002/9781444338386.wbeah24167.

"Bog Butter Mystery Solved?" 4 Feb. 2004, Archived from the original on 19 July 2011, https://web.archive.org/web/20110719140902/http://www.show.me.uk/site/news/STO269.html.

Brumm, Adam, Adhi Agus Oktaviana, Basran Burhan, Budianto Hakim, Rustan Lebe, Jian-xin Zhao, Priyatno Hadi Sulistyarto, Marlon Ririmasse, Shinatria Adhityatama, Iwan Sumantri, and Maxime Aubert. "Oldest cave art found in Sulawesi." *Science Advances,* vol. 7, no. 3, 13 Jan. 2021, https://www.science.org/doi/10.1126/.

"Cahokia: America's Lost Metropolis." Directed and produced by Liz Gray, *BBC Worldwide,* 1998, Alexander Street, https://video.alexanderstreet.com/watch/cahokia-america-s-lost-metropolis.

Chung, Young Yang. *Silken threads: a history of embroidery in China, Korea, Japan, and Vietnam.* H.N. Abrams, 2005, pp. 294, https://www.worldcat.org/title/silken-threads-a-history-of-embroidery-in-china-korea-japan-and-vietnam/oclc/55019211.

"Delphi: Place of Peaceful Conflict." *Films On Demand,* Films Media Group, 2006, fod.infobase.com/PortalPlaylists.aspx?wID=102632&xtid=38805.

Dempsy, Judy. "A 3,500-Year-Old Queen Causes a Rift Between Germany and Egypt". *The New York Times,* 18 Oct. 2009, https://www.nytimes.com/2009/10/19/world/europe/19iht-germany.html.

Dietrich, O., Heun, M., Notroff, J., Schmidt, K., and Zarnkow, M. "The role of cult and feasting in the emergence of neolithic communities. new evidence from göbekli tepe, south-eastern turkey." *Antiquity,* vol. 86, no. 33, 2012, pp. 674-695. doi:10.1017/S0003598X00047840.

Dugger, Celia W. and John Noble Wilford. "New Hominid Species Discovered in South Africa." *The New York Times,* 8 Apr. 2010. https://www.nytimes.com/2010/04/09/science/09fossil.html.

"Easter Island in Context: From Paradise to Calamity." *Films On Demand,* Films Media Group, 2002, fod.infobase.com/PortalPlaylists.aspx?wID=102632&xtid=30091.

"Emperor's Ghost Army." *Films On Demand,* Films Media Group, 2014, fod.infobase.com/PortalPlaylists.aspx?wID=102632&xtid=93464.

"First Peoples: Australia." *Films On Demand,* Films Media Group, 2015, fod.infobase.com/PortalPlaylists.aspx?wID=102632&xtid=129847.

Gansell, Amy Rebecca. "Identity and Adornment in the Third-Millennium Bc Mesopotamian 'Royal Cemetery' at Ur." *Cambridge Archaeological Journal,* vol. 17, no. 1, 2007, pp. 29–46, doi:10.1017/S0959774307000042.

"Germany to return looted Benin Bronzes to Nigeria in 2022". *Deutsche Welle English,* 29 April 2021.

"Great Zimbabwe." *Films On Demand,* Films Media Group, 2009, fod.infobase.com/PortalPlaylists.aspx?wID=102632&xtid=43766.

Gresky, Julia, Juliane Haelm, and Lee Clare. "Modified human crania from Göbekli Tepe provide evidence for a new form of Neolithic skull cult." *Science Advances,* vol 3, iss 6, 2017, https://www.science.org/doi/10.1126/sciadv.1700564.

Henson, Donald. *Doing Archaeology : A Subject Guide for Students.* Taylor & Francis Group, 2012.

Hill, Erica. "Archaeology and Animal Persons: Toward a Prehistory of Human-Animal Relations". *Environment and Society,* vol. 4, no. 1, 2013. doi:10.3167/ares.2013.040108.

Horvath, Agnes and Arpad Szakolczai. "Gobekli Tepe: Sanctuary as trickster bestiary, or the revival of transgression." *Walking into the Void,* Routledge, 2017.

"Ice Mummies: Siberian Ice Maiden". *PBS – NOVA,* https://www.pbs.org/wgbh/nova/transcripts/2517siberian.html.

Jeon, H.-T. "Artistic Creation, Borrowing, Adaptation, and Assimilation in Koguryo Tomb Murals of the Fourth to Seventh Century." *Archives of Asian Art,* vol 56, pp. 81-104, 2006, doi: 10.1484/aaa.2006.0005.

Kingsland, Kaitlyn. "Animal Crossing: New Horizons, Museums, and Cultural Heritage." *Archaeogaming.com,* 23 Mar 2020, https://archaeogaming.com/2020/03/23/animal-crossing-new-horizons-museums-and-cultural-heritage/.

Ledger, Paul M, Linus Girdland-Flink, and Véronique Forbes. "New horizons at L'Anse aux Meadows." *Proceedings of the National Academy of Sciences,* vol. 116, no. 31, Jul. 2019, doi: 10.1073/pnas.1907986116.

Lipo, Carl P., Terry L. Hunt, and Sergio Rapu Haoa. "The 'walking' megalithic statues (*moai*) of Easter Island." *Journal of Archaeological Science,* vol. 40, iss. 6, 2013, https://doi.org/10.1016/j.jas.2012.09.029.

Lusher, Adam. "British museums may loan Nigeria bronzes that were stolen from Nigeria by British imperialists". *The Independent,* 24 June 2018, https://www.independent.co.uk/news/uk/home-news/benin-bronzes-british-museum-nigeria-stolen-imperialist-treasures-return-loan-elgin-marbles-looted-a8414661.html.

Marchant, Jo. *The Shadow King: The Bizarre Afterlife of King Tut's Mummy*. Da Capo Press, 2013.

Maugh, Thomas H. II. "King Tut's Mundane Death: Malaria and a Broken Leg, Not Murder, Likely Led to His Demise, New Research Suggests." *Los Angeles Times,* 17 Feb. 2010, https://www.latimes.com/archives/la-xpm-2010-feb-17-la-sci-king-tut17-2010feb17-story.html.

McGlone, Peggy. "Smithsonian to give back its collection of Benin bronzes." *Washington Post,* 8 March 2022, https://www.washingtonpost.com/arts-entertainment/2022/03/08/smithsonian-benin-bronzes-nigeria-return/

Moore, Tristana. "Row over Nefertiti bust continues." *BBC News,* 7 May 2007, http://news.bbc.co.uk/1/hi/world/europe/6632021.stm.

"Nazca Decoded." *Films On Demand,* Films Media Group, 2009, fod.infobase.com/PortalPlaylists.aspx?wID=102632&xtid=52300.

Nichols, D.L. "Teotihuacan." *J Archaeol Res,* vol. 24, pp. 1–74, Mar 2016, https://doi.org/10.1007/s10814-015-9085-0.

Pain, Stephanie. "Arrow points to foul play in ancient iceman's death." *NewScientistTech,* 26 July 2001, archived from the original 23 August 2014, https://www.newscientist.com/article/dn1080-arrow-points-to-foul-play-in-ancient-icemans-death/.

Pitts, Mike. "The Henge Builders." *Archaeology,* vol. 61, no. 1, 2008, https://archive.archaeology.org/0801/etc/henge.html.

Pobojewski, Sally. "Underwater Storage Techniques Preserved Meat for Early Hunters." *The University Record,* 8 May 1995, https://www.ur.umich.edu/9495/May08_95/storage.htm.

Schemm, Paul. "A frail King Tut died from malaria, broken leg." *Newsday,* The Associated Press, 16 Feb. 2010, https://www.newsday.com/news/world/a-frail-king-tut-died-from-malaria-broken-leg-g53915.

"Secrets of Stonehenge." Directed by Gail Willumsen, produced by Melanie Wallace, et al., *Public Broadcasting Service,* 2010, Alexander Street, https://video.alexanderstreet.com/watch/secrets-of-stonehenge."

"Secrets of The Island of Minos: Secrets of Archaeology." *Films On Demand,* Films Media Group, 2003, fod.infobase.com/PortalPlaylists.aspx?wID=102632&xtid=76903.

"The Age of Heroes: Treasures of Ancient Greece." *Films On Demand,* Films Media Group, 2015, fod.infobase.com/PortalPlaylists.aspx?wID=102632&xtid=95223.

"The Vinland Mystery." Directed by William Pettigrew, produced by William Pettigrew and National Film Board of Canada, *National Film Board of Canada,* 1984, Alexander Street, https://video.alexanderstreet.com/watch/the-vinland-mystery.

Turner, Bethany L. and Armelagos, George J. "Diet, residential origin, and pathology at Machu Picchu, Peru". *American Journal of Physical Anthropology,* vol. 149, no. 1, pp. 71–83, 1 Sept. 2012, doi:10.1002/ajpa.22096.

Webster, D. "The archaeology of Copán, Honduras." *J Archaeol Res,* no. 7, pp. 1–53, Mar. 1999, https://doi-org.libproxy.lib.unc.edu/10.1007/BF02446084.

White, Shannon. "Treasures from the Royal Tombs of Ur: A Traveling Exhibition of the University of Pennsylvania Museum of Archaeology and Anthropology." *Near Eastern Archaeology,* vol. 67, no. 4, 2004.

Yellowstone National Park. "Atomic Elements and Archeology: Tracing Ancient Resource Access and Trade Routes Using XRF." *National Park Service,* 31 July 2019, https://www.nps.gov/teachers/classrooms/archeology-and-x-ray-fluorescence-xrf.htm.

ACKNOWLEDGMENTS

Thank you to my professors in the Classics and Anthropology/Archaeology departments at the University of North Carolina at Chapel Hill, whose course content and passion in their fields inspired me to choose certain sites and write this book.

These professors are: collaborators Dr. Benjamin S. Arbuckle and Dr. Hérica Valladares, Dr. Jennifer Gates-Foster, Dr. Al Duncan, Dr. Emily Baragwanath, and Dr. Laurie Cameron Steponaitis.

Great thanks to Dr. Jennifer Gates-Foster for also sharing her expertise on artifact ownership, and to Amanda Ball for archaeological content insights.

Special thanks for permissions to Archaeology Southwest and the Choctaw Nation of Oklahoma.

PHOTO CREDITS

Cover logo (throughout): SS/Victor Metelskiy (trowel); SS/domnitsky (sand)
Words to Remember (throughout): SS/Victor Metelskiy
Archaeological site journal page (throughout): SS/javarman
Arrows (throughout): SS/TWINS DESIGN STUDIO
Front Cover: SS/SCStock (background); SS/AD Hunter (mag glass)
Back Cover: SS/AlexAnton (background); SS/Microgen (person); SS/ f11photo (top R); SS/Mr Nai (below top R); SS/WitR (above bottom R); ©User:kevinmcgill/https://www.flickr.com/photos/kevinamcgill/6143564816/WC/CC BY-SA 2.0/https://creativecommons.org/licenses/by-sa/2.0/deed.en/No changes made (bottom R)
Map: SS/Kitnha (background); SS/Wangkun Jia (Teotihuacan); SS/Russ Heinl (L'Anse); SS/Kent Raney (Cahokia); SS/Daniel Prudek (Nazca); SS/milosk50 (Copan); SS/Leonid Andronov (Tikal); SS/Amy Nichole Harris (Easter); SS/SCStock (Machu); SS/Georgios Tsichlis (Knossos); SS/Mr Nai (Stonehenge); SS/allouphoto (Woodhenge); SS/trabantos (Delphi); SS/WitR (Pompeii); iStock/JoseIgnacioSoto (Tut); SS/evenfh (Zimbabwe); iStock/Ustman Amrulloh Alha (Sulawesi); SS/mehmet.ozer (Gobekli); SS/Rasool Ali (Ur); ©Richard Mortel/flickr/CC BY 2.0/https://creativecommons.org/licenses/by/2.0/No changes made (Pazyryk); ©User:Jmhullot/WC/CC BY-SA 3.0/https://creativecommons.org/licenses/by-sa/3.0/deed.en/No changes made (Terracotta); WC/PD-US (Anak); SS/Dmitry Rukhlenko (Bayon); SS/Leah-Anne Thompson (Mungo)
Timeline: SS/bluefish_ds (background); SS/Wangkun Jia (Teotihuacan); SS/Russ Heinl (L'Anse); SS/Kent Raney (Cahokia); SS/Daniel Prudek (Nazca); SS/milosk50 (Copan); SS/Leonid Andronov (Tikal); SS/Amy Nichole Harris (Easter); SS/SCStock (Machu); SS/Georgios Tsichlis (Knossos); SS/Mr Nai (Stonehenge); SS/allouphoto (Woodhenge); SS/trabantos (Delphi); SS/WitR (Pompeii); iStock/JoseIgnacioSoto (Tut); SS/evenfh (Zimbabwe); iStock/Ustman Amrulloh Alha (Sulawesi); SS/mehmet.ozer (Gobekli); SS/Rasool Ali (Ur); ©Richard Mortel/flickr/CC BY 2.0/https://creativecommons.org/licenses/by/2.0/No changes made (Pazyryk); ©User:Jmhullot/WC/CC BY-SA 3.0/https://creativecommons.org/licenses/by-sa/3.0/deed.en/No changes made (Terracotta); WC/PD-US (Anak); SS/Dmitry Rukhlenko (Bayon); SS/Leah-Anne Thompson (Mungo)
2-3: SS/Stone background
3: SS/evenfh (Zimbabwe); SS/WitR (Pompeii); SS/Wangkun Jia (Teotihuacan)
5: SS/Amy Nichole Harris
6: SS/John Kepchar (arrowhead); SS/AD Hunter (mag glass)
7: SS/SCStock (background); SS/Andrew Krasovitckii (timeline)
8-9: SS/averych
8: SS/Frogella (bubble); SS/Massimo Todaro (top L); SS/Karl Allen Lugmayer (top R); ©Look and Learn (middle L); SS/Macrovector (bottom L); SS/Viacheslav Lopatin (bottom R)
10: SS/motestockphoto (dirt); SS/John Kepchar (arrowhead); SS/AD Hunter (mag glass); SS/bonchan (book)
11: SS/Microgen
12-13: SS/3523studio
12: SS/AD Hunter (mag glass); ©User:PI3.124/WC/CC BY-SA 4.0/https://creativecommons.org/licenses/by-sa/4.0/deed.en/No Changes Made (artifacts); SS/Anton_Ivanov (features L); SS/kccullenPhoto (features R); SS/Jerome Stubbs (features bottom); SS/Don Laught (ecofacts L); SS/Neils Oscategui Mallqui (ecofacts R)
14-15: SS/SCStock (background); SS/Sanit Fuangnakhon (llama); SS/Chiociolla (icons)
16-17: SS/SCStock
16: SS/Openfinal
17: iStock/Mypurgatoryyears (L); SS/cornfield (top R); ©Wolfgang Holzem/https://ehalal.io/WC/CC BY 3.0/https://creativecommons.org/licenses/by/3.0/deed.en/No changes made (bottom R)
18: SS/Andrey Armyagov
19: SS/dmitry_islentev (trees and hands); SS/Pakhnyushchy (aerial); SS/StanislavBeloglazov (photographer); SS/Leonid Andronov (Tikal); ©Juan Carlos Fernandez Diaz/National Center for Airborne Laser Mapping (LiDAR)
20-21: SS/Daniel Prudek (background); SS/Lenka Pribanova (spiral); SS/John Kershner (hummingbird); SS/Robert CHG (condor); SS/Rainer Lesniewski (icons)
22: SS/Microgen (background); SS/inspired-fiona (graph)
23: SS/krugloff (top R); SS/VicVa (L); SS/Chiyacat (middle); SS/Victor Martin Dorronsoro (R)
24: ©Rice University & OpenStax/CC BY 4.0/https://creativecommons.org/licenses/by/4.0/No changes made (top); SS/JeannieR (L); ©Carmen Sarjeant/WC/CC BY-SA 4.0/https://creativecommons.org/licenses/by-sa/4.0/deed.en/No changes made (R)
25: SS/Kent Raney (Cahokia); ©Herb Roe/WC/CC BY-SA 3.0/https://creativecommons.org/licenses/by-sa/3.0/deed.en/No changes made (layers); ©Thank You (21 Millions+) views/flickr/CC BY 2.0/https://creativecommons.org/licenses/by/2.0/No changes made (past Cahokia); SS/Microgen (L); SS/stockphotofan1 (middle); SS/Zichrini (R)
26-27: SS/Matt Gush (background); SS/bsd studio (icons)
28: SS/OlgaChernyak (camera); SS/inspired-fiona (graph); SS/WilliamPol (Munsell); SS/funnyangel (texture); ©Craig McCaa, Bureau of Land Management Alaska/flickr/CC BY 2.0/https://creativecommons.org/licenses/by/2.0/No changes made (backfilling); iStock/microgen (bottom)
29: SS/krugloff (top L); iStock/Mypurgatoryyears (top R); SS/irmaamri (bottom L); SS/Everyonephoto Studio (bottom R)
30: SS/W. Scott McGill (arrowheads); SS/Elvira Tursynbayeva (pottery)
31: SS/VanoVasaio (top R); ©Chirikure et al./https://doi.org/10.1371/journal.pone.0178335/CC BY 4.0/https://creativecommons.org/licenses/by/4.0/No changes made (plate); SS/evenfh (Zimbabwe)
32: ©The Portable Antiquities Scheme/The Trustees of the British Museum/WC/CC BY-SA 4.0/https://creativecommons.org/licenses/by-sa/4.0/deed.en/No changes made (XRF coin); ©The Portable Antiquities Scheme/The Trustees of the British Museum/WC/CC BY-SA 2.0/https://creativecommons.org/licenses/by-sa/2.0/deed.en/No changes made (XRF zoom); Danita Delimont/Alamy Stock Photo (mummy and scan); ©User:Orlandata/https://www.entitree.com/en/family_tree/Tutankhamun/CC BY-SA 4.0/https://creativecommons.org/licenses/by-sa/4.0/deed.en/No changes made (family)
33: SS/Anna69 (L); SS/mountainpix (R); iStock/JoseIgnacioSoto (Tut)
34-35: SS/Cube29
36: ©Rice University & OpenStax/CC BY 4.0/https://creativecommons.org/licenses/by/4.0/No Changes Made (top); SS/Tim photo-video (middle); Fadil Aziz/Alcibbum Photograph/Getty Images (bottom)
37: SS/Russ Heinl (top); iStock/Ustman Amrulloh Alha (bottom)
38: SS/AD Hunter (mag glass); SS/OlgaChernyak (shovel); SS/bonchan (book); SS/mehmet.ozer (background); ©Sue Fleckney/flickr /CC BY-SA 2.0/https://creativecommons.org/licenses/by-sa/2.0/No changes made (bottom R)
39: SS/OlgaChernyak (shovel); SS/bonchan (book); ©User:Dosseman/WC/CC BY-SA 4.0/https://creativecommons.org/licenses/by-sa/4.0/deed.en/No changes made (top L); SS/AlicanA (top R); SS/cornfield (middle); ©User:Dosseman/WC/CC BY-SA 4.0/https://creativecommons.org/licenses/by-sa/4.0/deed.en/No changes made (bottom)
40: SS/Rasool Ali (background); ©User:Osama Shukir Muhammed Amin FRCP(Glasg)/WC/CC BY-SA 4.0/https://creativecommons.org/licenses/by-sa/4.0/deed.en/No changes made (L); ©British Museum/https://www.britishmuseum.org/collection/object/W_1928-1009-378/WC/CC BY-SA 4.0/https://creativecommons.org/licenses/by-sa/4.0/deed.en/No changes made (R)
41: SS/OlgaChernyak (shovel); SS/bonchan (book); WC/PD-US (top and 3rd from top); ©User:JMiall/British Museum/WC/CC BY-SA 3.0/https://creativecommons.org/licenses/by-sa/3.0/deed.en/No changes made (below top); SS/Simon Edge (bottom)
42: SS/Mr Nai
43: SS/allouphoto (background); ©Rog Frost/Woodhenge at North Newnton/geograph.org.uk/WC/CC BY-SA 2.0/https://creativecommons.org/licenses/by-sa/2.0/deed.en/No changes made
44-45: SS/Valerie2000 (background); SS/JosepPerianes (icons)
47: SS/Simon Edge (ziggurat); SS/Intellson (computer); SS/Antony McAulay (Vesta L); ©A derivative work of a 3D model by Lasha Tskhondia-L.VII.C./WC/CC BY-SA 3.0/https://creativecommons.org/licenses/by-sa/3.0/deed.en/No changes made (Vesta R); ©Camelia.boban/WC/CC BY-SA 3.0/https://creativecommons.org/licenses/by-sa/3.0/No changes made (Fortuna L); SS/McCarony (Fortuna R)
48: ©Wolfgang Holzem/https://ehalal.io/WC/CC BY 3.0/https://creativecommons.org/licenses/by/3.0/deed.en/No changes made (L); SS/Alan Ochieng (R)
49: SS/Claudio Divizia (top L); SS/Egabor8 (top R); ©User:Joyofmuseums/WC/CC BY-SA 4.0/https://creativecommons.org/licenses/by-sa/4.0/deed.en/No changes made (middle R); ©User:Michel wal/British Museum/WC/CC BY-SA 3.0/https://creativecommons.org/licenses/by-sa/3.0/deed.en/No changes made (bottom R); SS/THINK A (bottom)
50: ©User:hyolee2/WC/CC BY-SA 3.0/https://creativecommons.org/licenses/by-sa/3.0/deed.en/No changes made (L); ©User:Lemurbaby/WC/CC BY-SA 3.0/https://creativecommons.org/licenses/by-sa/3.0/deed.en/No changes made (R)
51: SS/Leah-Anne Thompson (background); The Natural History Museum/Alamy Stock Photo (Mungo Man)
52-53: SS/AlexAnton (dry desert); SS/Anda Mikelsone (wet bog); SS/Kertu (frozen land); ©User:Bazonka/WC/CC BY-SA 3.0/https://creativecommons.org/licenses/by-sa/3.0/deed.en/No changes made (bog butter); ©Allan Henderson/flickr/CC BY 2.0/https://creativecommons.org/licenses/by/2.0/No changes made (Otzi)

QR CODE CREDITS

ABOUT THE AUTHOR

Caitlin Sockin is an author and Assistant Publisher at WunderMill Books' Persnickety Press. Caitlin holds dual degrees in Archaeology and Classics from the University of North Carolina at Chapel Hill. Her interest in archaeology and classics began at a very young age, with her first museum visits and fascination with Egyptian pharaohs and deities. She created *Dig It!* to inspire kids to explore ancient history as it relates to their own lives, and potentially pursue archaeological interests as a hobby or career.

ABOUT THE COLLABORATORS

Benjamin S. Arbuckle is a professor in the Department of Anthropology at the University of North Carolina at Chapel Hill. He received his PhD in Archaeology from Harvard University. Dr. Arbuckle studies the ancient history and prehistory of Southwestern Asia and carries a special passion for exploring human-animal relationships, including the hidden histories of the animals that live closest to us—pets, livestock, and "vermin."

Hérica Valladares is an associate professor of Classics at the University of North Carolina at Chapel Hill, where she teaches courses on the art and archaeology of the ancient Mediterranean. She is a faculty member of UNC's Curriculum in Archaeology and serves as the Chair of the Academic Advisory Council for the Ackland Art Museum. Her book, *Painting, Poetry, and the Invention of Tenderness in the Early Roman Empire*, was published by Cambridge University Press in 2021.

DIG IT!